Careers in Focus

FASHION
THIRD EDITION

FASHION

THIRD EDITION

Ferguson

An imprint of Infobase Publishing

Careers in Focus: Fashion, Third Edition

Copyright © 2007 by Infobase Publishing

Ferguson
An imprint of Infobase Publishing
132 West 31st Street
New York NY 10001

Library of Congress Cataloging-in-Publication Data

Careers in focus. Fashion. — 3rd ed.
   p.cm.
  Includes index.
  ISBN 0-8160-6563-2 (hc : alk. paper)
   1. Fashion—Vocational guidance. 2. Clothing trade— Vocational guidance.
I. J.G. Ferguson Publishing Company.
TT507.C337 2006
746.9'2003—dc22

2006008401

Ferguson books are available at special discounts when purchased in bulk quantities for businesses, associations, institutions, or sales promotions. Please call our Special Sales Department in New York at (212) 967-8800 or (800) 322-8755.

You can find Ferguson on the World Wide Web at http://www.fergpubco.com

Text design by David Strelecky

Printed in the United States of America

MP DS 10 9 8 7 6 5 4 3 2 1

This book is printed on acid-free paper.

Table of Contents

Introduction 1
Apparel Industry Workers 6
Color Analysts and Image Consultants 18
Cosmetologists 28
Costume Designers 40
Fashion Buyers and Merchandisers 49
Fashion Coordinators 56
Fashion Designers 64
Fashion Illustrators 79
Fashion Model Agents 85
Fashion Photographers 93
Fashion Stylists 101
Fashion Writers and Editors 110
Jewelers and Jewelry Repairers 117
Knit Goods Industry Workers 127
Makeup Artists 136
Models 143
Nail Technicians 156
Shoe Industry Workers 167
Tailors and Dressmakers 176
Textile Workers 184
Index 195

Introduction

People have always needed clothes. In primitive times, clothing only served as a means of warmth and protection from the elements. Later civilizations began to produce more elaborate fabrics and from these fabrics made more ornate clothing. Yet the importance of clothing still centered on its functionality, which was reflected in clothing design and production. Over the centuries, as societies—and economies—became more established, clothing began to satisfy more complex needs. People began using clothing to express their personalities, indicate their rank or social standing, and enhance their looks. By the early 20th century the manufacturing of clothes had become the booming industry of fashion.

In the United States, New York City quickly became the country's fashion industry headquarters due to its proximity to the woolen mills of New England and the cotton mills of the South. More importantly, however, were the city's inexpensive workforces in the form of immigrant workers.

During the middle and later half of the 20th century, designers broadened their focus from creating only expensive and glamorous fashions (called haute couture) to designing ready-to-wear collections. This trend allowed more people access to fashion, since such clothing was less expensive and more practical.

Workers in many industries help to create the fashions we wear for business and pleasure.

Textiles. The textile industry produces fabrics for clothing, as well as fabrics for home furnishings, carpeting, towels, and sheets; ribbons, webbings, and tapes for automobile seat belts and conveyor belts; textiles for parachutes, fire-resistant and bullet-resistant uniforms; and fabrics for disposable surgical masks, gowns, and sheets, among other products. The textile industry is the largest manufacturing industry in the United States, with approximately 489,000 employees. The industry is also one of the most diversified, employing people from numerous racial, ethnic, and economic backgrounds. Employees work in three major categories: research and development, production, and merchandising.

Apparel. The apparel industry produces almost all types of clothing for men, women, and children and is made up of thousands of manufacturers. Nearly every important apparel manufacturer has a sales office in New York City. This is where large retailers send their buyers and where industry-wide sales meetings are held each new season. In addition to their New York offices, apparel companies often contract much of their production to foreign workers to cut down on production and labor costs. A large number of the apparel industry workers are women and minorities, accounting for almost a third of the workforce. Approximately 358,000 people are employed in this industry in the United States.

Design/marketing/support. This industry supports numerous workers with a variety of responsibilities. *Fashion designers* create new styles of clothing and accessories. These new styles are marketed and advertised via print publications, the Internet, and fashion shows. *Fashion coordinators* organize fashion shows to help designers market their products. They negotiate with *fashion model agents,* who represent *models* displaying new products at fashion shows and in print and electronic venues. *Cosmetologists, nail technicians,* and *makeup artists* help models to look their best when they market new fashions. *Fashion illustrators, photographers, and stylists* are responsible for creating a look for the products at the shows or in print, media, and other advertisements.

Fashion is constantly in flux, influenced by such factors as international styles as well as the costs of production. In the face of foreign competition, the future of the fashion industry in the United States is unclear. The popularity of imported work from foreign countries has deeply affected the U.S. apparel and textile industries, decreasing U.S. manufacturers' share of the U.S. market. In addition, a provision of the North Atlantic Free Trade Agreement provides for apparel made in Mexico and Canada to be imported duty-free into the United States. As a result, many U.S. companies have moved their operations across these borders to reduce production costs. Offshore assembly is also a practice that is expected to affect the employment of U.S. workers. In the offshore assembly process, workers from Caribbean countries assemble pieces of fabric that were cut in the United States. The finished product is then imported back into the United States—all at a much lower cost to the manufacturer. As a result of all of these developments, employment in U.S. textile and apparel manufacturing plants has declined and may continue in this direction.

Despite this decline, however, improvements such as new spinning and weaving methods, better printing processes, and increased adaptation of computers to manufacturing operations have made the textile and apparel industries more efficient and productive. As new machines and methods are developed and put into place, technical jobs will increase, and less skilled, machine-operating jobs will decrease. Because smaller companies cannot afford to make extensive technological changes, some are forced to merge with larger companies. The result is a consolidation of large corporations rather than the many small firms of years ago.

Recent concerns for the environment have led to efforts to reduce the amount of pollution generated by manufacturing plants. For the textile industry, environmental awareness can mean taking steps such as changing ingredients in a chemical used for dyeing, building a water-purification system, making a financial contribution for the construction of a municipal waste-treatment facility, or studying the recycling of liquids. In the future, there will be an increased demand for people who are trained to protect the natural environment.

The fastest growth in fashion retail is projected for apparel and accessory stores. The market for custom-made clothing is declining as consumers buy more mass-produced apparel. Despite this, the best opportunities for apparel workers are available to the highly skilled. Tailors and dressmakers whose skills are specialized and still necessary in some retail stores, laundries, and dry cleaners will have better opportunities than most apparel workers.

Opportunities should be better for workers in the creative side of the industry, such as designers, photographers, and stylists. But competition for these exciting and rewarding careers will be strong.

Each article in this book discusses a particular fashion occupation in detail. The articles in *Careers in Focus: Fashion* appear in Ferguson's *Encyclopedia of Careers and Vocational Guidance,* but have been updated and revised with the latest information from the U.S. Department of Labor, professional organizations, and other sources. The following paragraphs detail the sections and features that appear in the book.

The **Quick Facts** section provides a brief summary of the career, including recommended school subjects, personal skills, work environment, minimum educational requirements, salary ranges, certification or licensing requirements, and employment outlook. This section also provides acronyms and identification numbers for the following government classification indexes: the *Dictionary of Occupational Titles* (DOT), the *Guide to Occupational Exploration* (GOE), the National Occupational Classification (NOC) Index, and the Occupational Information Network (O*NET)-Standard Occupational Classification System (SOC) index. The DOT, GOE, and O*NET-SOC indexes have been created by the U.S. government; the NOC index is Canada's career-classification system. Readers can use the identification numbers listed in the Quick Facts section to access further information about a career. Print editions of the DOT (*Dictionary of Occupational Titles.* Indianapolis, Ind: JIST

Works, 1991) and GOE (*The Guide for Occupational Exploration*. 3d ed. Indianapolis, Ind.: JIST Works, 2001) are available at libraries. Electronic versions of the NOC (http://www23.hrdc-drhc. gc.ca) and O*NET-SOC (http://online.onetcenter.org) are available on the World Wide Web. When no DOT, GOE, NOC, or O*NET-SOC numbers are present, this means that the U.S. Department of Labor or Human Resources Development Canada have not created a numerical designation for this career. In this instance, you will see the acronym "N/A," or not available.

The **Overview** section is a brief introductory description of the duties and responsibilities involved in this career. Oftentimes, a career may have a variety of job titles. When this is the case, alternative career titles are presented.

The **History** section describes the history of the particular job as it relates to the overall development of its industry or field.

The Job describes the primary and secondary duties of the job.

Requirements discusses high school and postsecondary education and training requirements, any certification or licensing that is necessary, and other personal requirements for success in the job.

Exploring offers suggestions on how to gain experience in or knowledge of the particular job before making a firm educational and financial commitment. The focus is on what can be done while still in high school (or in the early years of college) to gain a better understanding of the job.

The **Employers** section gives an overview of typical places of employment for the job.

Starting Out discusses the best ways to land that first job, be it through the college placement office, newspaper ads, or personal contact.

The **Advancement** section describes what kind of career path to expect from the job and how to get there.

Earnings lists salary ranges and describes the typical fringe benefits.

The **Work Environment** section describes the typical surroundings and conditions of employment—whether indoors or outdoors, noisy or quiet, social or independent. Also discussed are typical hours worked, any seasonal fluctuations, and the stresses and strains of the job.

The **Outlook** section summarizes the job in terms of the general economy and industry projections. For the most part, Outlook information is obtained from the U.S. Bureau of Labor Statistics and is supplemented by information taken from professional associations. Job growth terms follow those used in the *Occupational Outlook*

Handbook. Growth described as "much faster than the average" means an increase of 36 percent or more. Growth described as "faster than the average" means an increase of 21 to 35 percent. Growth described as "about as fast as the average" means an increase of 10 to 20 percent. Growth described as "more slowly than the average" means an increase of 3 to 9 percent. Growth described as "little or no change" means an increase of 0 to 2 percent. "Decline" means a decrease of 1 percent or more.

Each article ends with **For More Information,** which lists organizations that provide information on training, education, internships, scholarships, and job placement.

Careers in Focus: Fashion also includes photos, informative sidebars, and interviews with professionals in the field.

Apparel Industry Workers

OVERVIEW

Apparel industry workers produce, maintain, or repair clothing and other consumer products made from cloth, leather, or fur. The three basic processes of garment production are cutting, sewing, and pressing. According to the U.S. Department of Labor, there are approximately 1.1 million textile, apparel, and furnishings workers. Apparel industry employees work primarily in manufacturing firms, though some are employed in retail establishments or laundries and dry-cleaners. They may be involved in creating apparel, from working with the pattern to cutting or sewing together parts of a garment through the final stages of finishing or inspecting the item.

HISTORY

The first sewing machine was patented in Paris in 1830 by Barthelemy Thimonnier. But weavers and tailors, fearful of being driven out of business by the mass production machines, destroyed the factories where the work was taking place, causing instances of violence across Europe.

The history of apparel workers in the United States is intertwined with the history of the early American labor movement. In 1846 Elias Howe patented a sewing machine in the United States that used two threads in a lock stitch pattern, as sewing machines use today. However, the Howe sewing machine was no more accepted in the United States than Thimonnier's invention had been in Paris, and Howe sold part of the patent rights in England.

In 1851 Isaac Singer built a sewing machine that survived the objections of the tailors. The machine only made simple stitches, and tailors would still be needed for much of the work on clothing. The machine would speed production of the basic elements of garments. Workers were required to purchase their own sewing machines.

As the industrial revolution progressed, the sewing machine was joined in 1860 by a band-knife cutting machine, invented by John Barran of Leeds, England, that cut several layers of fabric. In the 1890s, the first spreading machine was put to use in garment making, as was the first buttonhole machine, invented in the United States at the Reece Machinery Company. Factories replaced craft shops.

In the early 20th century, New York City became the largest producer of clothing in the world. The small factories that sprang up during these early decades were poorly lit and ventilated, unsafe, and unsanitary. The rooms were packed with workers who labored 12 or 14 hours a day for meager wages. The term "sweatshop" came into being as a description of the apparel factories. On March 25, 1911, in New York City, a disastrous fire swept through the Triangle Shirtwaist Factory, killing 145 people, most of them young girls employed in the factory.

As a direct result of the tragedy, the city was forced to revise its building codes and labor laws, and membership in unions working in the apparel industry increased dramatically. The International Ladies' Garment Workers' Union, founded in 1900, developed enough support after the fire to lobby for labor laws to be enacted and enforced. The Amalgamated Clothing Workers of America was established in 1914 and soon became one of the largest unions in the apparel industry.

In 1995 the International Ladies' Garment Workers' Union and the Amalgamated Clothing and Textiles Union combined to form UNITE (Union of Needle Trades Industrial and Textile Employees), located in New York City.

In early clothing factories each worker assembled and finished an entire garment. Since the 1940s, workers in the ready-to-wear apparel industry have operated in an assembly-line fashion with strict divisions of labor among employees. However, apparel-manufacturing firms are increasingly using modular manufacturing systems in which operators work together in a module or group.

The biggest change in the apparel industry in the last 50 years has been the migration of manufacturing jobs to Asia and other foreign markets. A substantial number of garments are made abroad because of the reduced cost of labor and taxes and technologically advanced, well-engineered factories. The quantity of clothing imported has increased by more than 300 percent in the late 20th and early 21st century. Employment in the apparel industry has risen slightly in the last few years but is expected to decline in the United States through 2012.

THE JOB

Apparel industry workers produce, maintain, or repair clothing and other consumer products made from cloth, leather, or fur. The three basic processes of garment production are cutting, sewing, and pressing.

Production of a garment begins after the designer's sample product has been shown to retail buyers and accepted by the merchandising department of the company. *Markers* make a paper pattern, usually with the aid of a computer. The pattern indicates cutting lines, buttonhole and pocket placement, pleats, darts, and other details. Computers also grade each pattern piece for several sizes. Then the pattern is ready for mass production. Small shops may combine two or more of the following operations into a single job.

Spreaders lay out bolts of cloth into exact lengths on the cutting table. Many layers of fabric are spread on the cutting table, depending on the quality and weight of the material and the number of products needed.

Cutters have a variety of responsibilities that may include spreading fabric, machine cutting, and hand cutting master patterns. A machine cutter follows the pattern outline on the cloth and cuts various garment pieces from layers of cloth. Using an electrical cutting machine, the cutter slices through all the layers at once. The cutting may be done by hand for expensive or delicate materials. A cutting mistake can ruin yards of material; therefore, cutters must be extremely careful when cutting out the pattern. Newer technology has been developed, so that computer-controlled marker-makers and cutters are often used. Computers allow for more precise information to be programmed into set patterns and more uniform shapes to be cut.

The cut pieces of cloth are prepared for the sewing room by *assemblers* who bring together various pieces needed, including lining, interfacing, and trimmings, to make a complete garment. They match color, size, and fabric design and use chalk or thread to mark locations of pockets, buttonholes, buttons, and other trimmings. They identify each bundle with a ticket. (This ticket was also used to figure the earnings of workers who were paid according to the number of pieces they produced. Present technology uses bar codes and computers to calculate the worker's pay and track the bundles through the production line.) The bundles are then sent to the sewing room.

Apparel industry workers must have good hand-eye coordination and the ability to perform repetitious tasks. *(Corbis)*

Sewers, who constitute 70 percent of all apparel workers, are responsible for attaching the cut pieces of fabric using sewing machines. These and other production workers must be careful to follow patterns supplied by the designers. *Sewing machine operators* usually perform specialized sewing operations, such as collars, hems, or bindings. Since a variety of sewing operations and machines are required for each product, workers are classified by the type of machine and specific product on which they work. Workers are categorized into those who produce clothing and those who produce such nongarment items as curtains, sheets, and towels.

Hand sewers are highly skilled workers who perform sewing operations on delicate or valuable materials. They may specialize in a particular operation, such as adding trim or lace or sewing buttonholes. Some hand sewers also assist the designer in producing a sample product.

After the sewing operations have been completed, workers remove loose threads, basting, stitching, and lint. The sewn product may be inspected at this time.

Pressers operate the automatic pressing machines. Some pressing is done as a garment is assembled; sometimes it is done at the completion of all sewing. Delicate garments must be pressed by hand. Pressers may specialize in a particular garment or final press finished garments before they are shipped to stores.

Apparel inspectors and *production control technicians* monitor all stages of the production process and keep materials flowing smoothly through the various departments. They may detect defects in uncut fabric so that the layout workers and markers can position the material to avoid the defects, or they may identify defects in semi-finished garments, which inspectors may mend themselves or send back to production for repair.

Inspected finished clothing is then sent to the shipping room. From there, the product is sent to the markets the manufacturer has created for the product.

Tailors make garments from start to finish and must be knowledgeable in all phases of clothing production. Custom tailors take measurements and assist the customer in selecting fabrics. Many tailors work in retail outlets where they make alterations and adjustments to ready-to-wear clothing.

Apparel manufacturers increasingly organize workers in groups or modules. Workers specialize in one operation but are cross-trained in the various operations performed within the module. This system allows operators to better communicate with other workers and take on responsibility for running the module, including scheduling, monitoring standards, and correcting problems. Production time is reduced, while product quality is increased.

Most manufacturers have small factories employing fewer than a hundred workers. Because many of these small firms lack the capital resources to invest in new, more efficient equipment, the nature of the work of many apparel workers has been relatively unaffected by increased use of technology. However, only 10 percent of all workers in the apparel and textile industries are self-employed. The relatively few companies employing more than 100 workers account for more than 60 percent of the work force. Some larger firms have modernized facilities with computerized operations and automated material handling systems.

REQUIREMENTS

High School

Few employers of apparel workers require a high school diploma or previous experience. However, high school courses in family and consumer science, sewing, and vocational training on machinery are helpful. Since computers increasingly are being used in many types of production, knowledge of them is advantageous.

A high school diploma is required for more technical positions involving computers. Mechanical drafting, design, and mathematics are excellent training, and communications classes may help you advance into supervisory or management positions.

Postsecondary Training

If you have secondary or postsecondary vocation training or work experience in apparel production, you usually have a better chance of getting a job and advancing to a supervisory position.

There are two-year associate's degrees offered at technical colleges and community colleges. Many of these degree programs offer internships or cooperative education sessions spent working as a paid employee of an apparel company. Some students attend school under the sponsorship of a clothing company and usually go to work for their sponsor after graduation. Some are cooperative students who attend school with the understanding that they will return to their sponsor company. Some employers, however, do not place any restriction on their co-op students and allow them to seek the best job they can find.

Apparel machinery operators usually are trained on the job by experienced employees or by machinery manufacturer's representatives. As apparel machinery becomes more complex, workers increasingly will require training in computers and electronics. The modular system's trend toward cross-training will increase operators' needs to learn different machines and increase their skills.

Other Requirements

A knowledge of fabrics and their characteristics as well as good hand-eye coordination and the ability to perform repetitious tasks is necessary for apparel workers. An interest in learning a variety of skills in the apparel trade provides a worker with more job options and security. You need to be able to work well with others and accept direction.

EXPLORING

High schools, vocational schools, or colleges may provide you with information about job opportunities in the apparel industry. Occupational information centers and catalogs of schools that offer programs for apparel technicians also are good sources of information. A visit to a clothing factory makes it possible to observe the machinery and activities and gives you an opportunity to talk to apparel workers and gain insight about the jobs. To test your aptitude for this work, you may also consider working on fabric projects yourself or joining an organization, such as 4-H, that offers such projects.

EMPLOYERS

Approximately 1.1 million textile, apparel, and furnishings workers are employed in the United States. Apparel industry workers are employed in many settings, from multinational corporations such as Levi Strauss to small companies with few employees. Production jobs are concentrated in California, New York, North Carolina, Pennsylvania, Tennessee, and Georgia, though small clothing manufacturers are located in many parts of the country. More than one-half of all pressers are employed in laundry and dry-cleaning businesses, which exist throughout the United States. This work does not require much prior training or experience. Only 10 percent of workers in this industry are self-employed; more than one-third of tailors, dressmakers, and sewers and more than one-quarter of upholsterers work for themselves. Custom tailors often work in retail clothing stores. Retailers prefer to hire custom tailors and sewers with previous experience in the apparel field. Hand sewers may find work adding trimming to a wide variety of apparel, from clothing to accessories.

STARTING OUT

If you are interested in working in the apparel industry, you may apply directly to apparel manufacturing firms. Jobs often are listed with state employment agencies, in newspaper classified ads, or in trade publications. Companies may also post openings on a sign outside the building. Local unions also may be good sources of job leads.

A small number of skilled workers such as tailors and patternmakers are trained in formal apprenticeship programs. Special courses in sewing, tailoring, and patternmaking are offered in apparel industry centers in New York City and parts of the South.

Many employers have a strong preference for graduates of the two-year program and give such graduates a short, intensive in-plant orientation and training program so they can be placed where their skills can be used immediately. Many graduate apparel technicians who have participated in a cooperative program are given responsible positions immediately upon graduation. Some in-plant training programs are designed to train new technicians to work as supervisors.

Custom tailors and sewers with experience in apparel manufacture are more likely to be hired by retailers. Knowledge of fabric design and construction is essential. Laundry and dry cleaning establishments often hire inexperienced workers. However, applicants with work experience are preferred.

ADVANCEMENT

Advancement for apparel workers is somewhat limited. Most apparel workers begin by performing simple tasks and are assigned more difficult operations as they gain experience. While most remain on the production line, some apparel production workers become first-line supervisors.

It doesn't take much time to acquire the skill of an experienced operator in most branches of the apparel industry. Though it takes many different operations to complete a garment, each individual step is relatively simple, and only a short training period is required for each one. In the men's clothing field and in the women's coat and suit field, however, more tailoring is necessary, and the learning period to become an experienced sewer or operator is longer.

To enter the cutting department, a person usually starts as a fabric spreader and then advances to machine cutting. After further experience is acquired, the worker may grade the master pattern for the sizes, lay out the patterns on the fabric or paper, and mark for the cutting of the fabric. These are skilled operations, and it takes some years to advance and become an experienced all-around cutter. However, the advantages of having acquired these skills are great, for a cutter can, without too much difficulty, transfer his or her cutting skill from one branch of the apparel industry to another. Cutters usually are the highest paid factory workers.

Patternmakers with design school training may become fashion designers.

Custom tailoring is a very competitive field. To be successful in their own shops, tailors need training and experience in small-business operations.

Opportunities for advancement are excellent for graduates of two-year apparel technician programs. They may become section supervisors, production superintendents, or plant managers. There are also opportunities to move into industrial engineering, quality control, production control, or specialized technical areas. Some technicians may become plant training specialists or plant safety experts and directors.

Graduates from regular engineering colleges or community colleges with applied engineering programs also have advantages in securing employment in the apparel industry. Such people may start their training as junior engineers or production assistants, but their advancement is usually rapid. Within a few years, they can achieve secure status in the industry and earn salaries at an executive level.

EARNINGS

The apparel industry is highly competitive, and low profits and wages are characteristic. According to the U.S. Department of Labor, sewing machine operators earned an average hourly wage of $8.67, or $18,030 a year, in 2004. Patternmakers and layout workers averaged $14.70 per hour (or $30,580 annually); pressers, $8.36 an hour (or $17,390 annually); and custom tailors, $11.06 an hour (or $23,010 annually). General salaries for workers in this field range from less than $15,000 to more than $36,000 annually. Many workers in the industry are paid according to the number of acceptable pieces they turn out; therefore, their total earnings also depend on their skill, accuracy, and speed.

Due to the seasonal nature of the apparel industry, production workers may have periods of unemployment. However, during slack periods firms usually reduce the number of working hours for all workers rather than lay off some workers.

Large apparel employers usually include health and life insurance coverage, paid holidays and vacations, and childcare. Small firms may offer only limited benefits. Unions also provide benefits to their members. Employees of some of the larger manufacturers who operate company stores may enjoy discounts of 10 to 30 percent on their purchases.

WORK ENVIRONMENT

Working conditions in apparel production vary by establishment and type of job. Older factories may be poorly lit and ventilated and may be congested. Modern facilities usually are more comfortable, better lit and ventilated, have more work space, and may even be carpeted. Patternmaking and spreading areas and retail stores are quiet, while sewing and pressing facilities often are noisy. Laundries and dry cleaning establishments frequently are hot and noisy.

Apparel workers generally work a 35-to-40 hour, five-day week. Except for sewing, the apparel manufacturing industry traditionally has involved several shifts and therefore requires some employees to work evenings or weekends. Some companies have two sewing shifts to offset the cost of expensive machinery. Laundry and dry cleaning and retail workers may work evening and weekend hours.

Apparel production work can be monotonous, repetitive, and physically demanding. Workers may sit or stand many hours, leaning over tables or operating machinery. However, the physical demand on apparel workers has decreased as new machinery and production techniques, such as footpedal or computer-controlled pressing machines, have been implemented. While apparel workers face no serious health hazards or dangers, they need to be attentive while operating such equipment as automated cutters, sewing machines, or pressers. Some workers must wear gloves or other protective attire or devices.

Emphasis on teamwork and cooperation is increasing in those areas of apparel production that employ a modular system. As the module or team often must manage itself, groups and individual sewing machine operators may be under pressure to improve their performance while maintaining quality.

OUTLOOK

Employment of apparel workers is expected to decline through 2012, according to the U.S. Department of Labor. Increased imports, use of offshore assembly, and greater productivity through the introduction of labor-saving machinery will reduce the demand for these workers.

However, hand sewing is expected to decrease far less than other areas of apparel work due to the complexity of these tasks and difficulties in performing them by machine. Workers who have cross-trained and are capable of performing several different functions have a better chance at remaining in the field during periods of decline. Also, many pre-sewing functions are expected to be performed domestically, so workers in this area will not be as adversely affected. Also, the market for luxury hand-produced clothes is expected to remain steady.

The sewing process is expected to remain relatively nonautomated. Machine operators will continue to perform most sewing functions, and automated sewing will be limited to simple tasks. Better sewing machines will increase the productivity of operators and significantly decrease the amount of time needed to train them. Other functions, such as training, also will see productivity increases and further reduce the demand for production workers.

Because of the large size of this occupation, many thousands of job openings will arise each year to replace workers who retire, leave, or transfer to other fields.

Employment in the domestic apparel industry has declined in recent years as foreign companies have become able to produce goods less expensively than the United States. Imports now account for roughly half the domestic apparel consumption. Imports are expected to increase as the U.S. market opens further due to the North American Free Trade Agreement (NAFTA), the Agreement on Textiles and Clothing (ATC) of the World Trade Organization, and the Caribbean Basin Initiative (CBI). NAFTA and the CBI allow apparel produced in Mexico and Canada to be imported duty free to the United States. Some apparel companies are expected to move their production facilities to Mexico to reduce costs. In addition, the implementation of the ATC has resulted in the elimination of quotas and a reduction in tariffs for many apparel products. As a result, domestic production has continued to move abroad and imports into the U.S. market have increased, causing further employment decline for apparel workers in the United States.

In those areas of apparel such as women's clothing, where market changes occur rapidly, domestic manufacturers can respond more quickly, giving them some advantage, especially in high-fashion items. Using computers and electronic data, manufacturers can keep retailers stocked with popular items and reduce production of those not selling well. However, the industry is changing in favor of large manufacturers who have more technology available than the smaller, less efficient companies. New technologies, such as computer-controlled processing and instrumentation, will require more technicians with computer skills.

As consumers increasingly prefer to buy new mass-produced apparel, the need for custom-made clothes, and thus for custom tailors and sewers, also will decline.

FOR MORE INFORMATION

For information on pop culture, latest fashion trends, and news in the industry, contact
American Apparel and Footwear Association
1601 North Kent Street, Suite 1200
Arlington, VA 22209
Tel: 800-520-2262
http://www.apparelandfootwear.org

For career information, visit the following website:
Career Threads
http://careerthreads.com

Color Analysts and Image Consultants

OVERVIEW

Color analysts assess their clients' coloring, including skin tone and hair and eye color, and teach them how to use their most flattering colors in clothing and makeup. *Image consultants* usually work with people in business, helping them present themselves in a professional manner.

Color and image consultants offer programs for individual women or men, for professional or social organizations, or for all the employees of one company. Some work with retailers, teaching salespersons about color and style and presenting in-store workshops.

HISTORY

In their book, *Color Me Beautiful's Looking Your Best,* Mary Spillane and Christine Sherlock cite a study by Albert Mehrabian. He found that the impression we make on others is made up of 55 percent appearance and behavior, 38 percent speech, and only 7 percent the content of what we say. These figures clearly show the importance of presenting yourself well in business, social, and other settings. Beauty consultants have been around for some time, but their work is constantly evolving. Because our society is increasingly mobile and we change jobs more often than our parents did, we are constantly establishing ourselves with new groups. In addition, television has increased our awareness of appearance and what it tells us about the individual. Projecting a positive image through our appearance and behavior helps us gain acceptance from social and business contacts, fit into the workplace, and meet the public.

In 1980, with the publication of Carole Jackson's book, *Color Me Beautiful,* many people, especially women, began to think of what they purchased and wore in a different way. No longer willing to accept whatever fashion decreed, they wanted colors and styles that enhanced their individual appearance. By the time more than 20 million people had read this *New York Times* bestseller, clothing manufacturers, cosmetic companies, and retailers felt the impact of the new consumer demand.

In the meantime, other businesses were dealing with their increased need for employees with technological backgrounds. Such employees often were totally involved in the technical aspects of their work and unconcerned about the impression they made on coworkers, clients, and the general public. Many companies began to provide training to help employees project better images, increasing the demand for image consultants.

THE JOB

Most color and image consultants are entrepreneurs, meaning that they own and manage their businesses and assume all the risks. They may work with individuals, groups, or both. Christine Sherlock, director of training and communications for Color Me Beautiful, reports that her firm trains color analysts in color and its use in wardrobe and makeup. Those who wish to become image consultants take additional training so they can help clients work on their overall appearance and grooming, as well as improve their voices, body language, and etiquette. Consultants also may learn to coach clients on dealing with the public and the media.

Susan Fignar, president of S. Fignar & Associates Inc., is a corporate image trainer and consultant who has been quoted in *Cosmopolitan*, the *Wall Street Journal*, and the *Chicago Tribune*. She works with some of the country's largest corporations and offers a variety of corporate programs and interactive workshops. Fignar says she provides training that helps people bring out their best personal and professional presence. Like other entrepreneurs, her business requires constant sales and marketing to obtain clients.

Her training sessions deal with such topics as making a good first impression, everyday etiquette, developing self-esteem and confidence, verbal communication, body language and facial expression, overall appearance, and appropriate dress for every occasion. She notices an increasing demand for her services in dress code consulting and training sessions on business casual dress.

Sherlock says consultants get satisfaction from helping others look better and feel good about themselves. "When a consultant helps a client with her wardrobe," she says, "the client not only saves money; she uses 100 percent of her wardrobe and no longer complains that she has nothing to wear."

REQUIREMENTS

High School

If you are interested in this work, you will benefit from taking classes and being involved in activities that develop your ability to communicate and increase your understanding of visual effects. Helpful classes to take include English, speech, and drama. Activities to consider participating in include drama clubs and debate teams. In drama club you may have the opportunity to help apply makeup, select wardrobes, and learn about the emotional impact appearances can have. Art classes are also helpful, especially classes that teach color theory. Since many people in this line of work are entrepreneurs, consider taking business, bookkeeping, or accounting classes, which will give you the knowledge you need to run your own business.

Any part-time job working with the public is also valuable experience. You can gain excellent experience from selling clothing or cosmetics in department stores, from working in beauty salons or spas, or from working as a waiter. Volunteer work that involves working with people will also help you hone your people skills.

Postsecondary Training

There are no formal, standardized training programs for color analysts and image consultants. In general, Susan Fignar recommends attending seminars or classes on color, psychology, training methods, and communications. She adds that a degree in liberal arts, with a major in education, is a plus for those working at the corporate level.

Color Me Beautiful has trainers who travel throughout the country. They offer people who wish to become consultants basic classes in skin care, makeup, and color analysis and advanced classes in such subjects as theory of style and presentation. Most classes take one or two days for a single topic; most working consultants take at least one new class each year.

If you get to know a color analyst or image consultant personally, you may be able to arrange an informal internship of your own.

Some people begin their careers in this field by working as apprentices to other consultants. Color Me Beautiful accepts a two-month apprenticeship with an approved consultant.

Certification or Licensing
The Association of Image Consultants International (AICI) provides three levels of certification: first level certification, certified image professional, and certified image master. Contact the AICI for more information.

Other Requirements
Christine Sherlock recommends this field for those who like to work with and help other people and says an interest in fashion and style are also obviously very helpful. A general flair for art and design would prove useful. Analysts and consultants should be friendly, outgoing, supportive of others, able to offer constructive feedback, and open to change. There are few disabilities that would prevent an individual from doing this work.

Susan Fignar believes experience in the business world, especially in management and public contact, is essential for corporate consulting. She says that corporate consultants must be mature, poised, and professional to have credibility, and that people are usually between the ages of 33 and 40 when they enter this field.

EXPLORING

One way to explore this career is to arrange for a personal visit to a consultant. The AICI, for example, offers lists of qualified consultants throughout the country (see the end of this article for contact information).

There are several books you can read to learn more about color and image consulting. Sherlock recommends *Color Me Beautiful* by Carole Jackson (Ballantine Books, 1987), *Color Me Beautiful's Looking Your Best: Color, Makeup, and Style* by Mary Spillane and Christine Sherlock (Madison Books, 2002), and *Women of Color* by Darlene Mathis (SPCK and Triangle, 1999). Fignar recommends *Image Consulting: The New Career* by Joan Timberlake (Acropolis Books, 1983), which discusses the various areas in which image consultants specialize. Because networking is so important in getting clients, she also suggests *Networlding: Building Relationships and Opportunities for Success* by Melissa Giovagnoli (Jossey-Bass, 2000). Local libraries should have additional books on color, fabrics, style, etiquette, and body language.

EMPLOYERS

For the most part, color analysts and image consultants are self-employed. They run their own consulting businesses, which allows them the freedom to decide what image consulting services they wish to offer. For example, some consultants concentrate on working with corporate clients; other consultants may also advise individuals. Consultants may get the products they sell from one company, such as Color Me Beautiful, or they may offer a range of products and services that provide ways for clients to feel good about themselves. Those in apprenticeships and consultants just entering the field may work for consultants who have already established their businesses.

STARTING OUT

Some consultants enter the field through apprenticeships. Fignar began by working in advertising, where she had extensive experience in meeting planning and often was responsible for company visitors. She eventually attended a training program on fashion and image consulting. She says there are many routes to entering this field.

ADVANCEMENT

Workers can advance from color analysts to image consultants to trainers by gaining experience and additional education. Sherlock began as an apprentice and has advanced through various positions with Color Me Beautiful. Salon and department store employees would advance along the path their employers have laid out.

Fignar hopes to expand her business by adding new clients, taking advantage of new trends, developing training for future image consultants, and forming alliances with consultants who offer related services. This is par for the course for all self-employed analysts and consultants. She has had her own business for seven years and says it takes three to five years to get a corporate consulting business established.

EARNINGS

A color analyst's or image consultant's earnings are determined by the number of hours the consultant works, the type of clientele served, and the consultant's location. Christine Sherlock says earnings are highest in New York City and southern California. Some consultants increase their incomes by offering additional services. Susan Fignar estimates that earnings start at under $20,000 but can reach $75,000 or more for top performers. Since many color analysts and image consultants own their own businesses, it may also be helpful to consider that some small business owners may earn only about $15,000 a year, while the most successful may make $100,000 or more. The Department of Labor reports that median annual earnings for beauticians and cosmetologists were $20,500 in 2004, with 10 percent making $13,100 or less and 10 percent making $37,140 or more.

Sherlock points out such advantages as owning your own business, flexible hours, controlling your own time, and opportunity for personal growth and development. Because most consultants are self-employed, they must provide their own insurance and other benefits.

WORK ENVIRONMENT

Many consultants work out of their homes. Color consultants also work in salons, boutiques, day spas, and retail areas. The work is indoors and may involve travel. Sherlock comments that the work has changed her life and that she loves everything she has done in the field.

Fignar works at corporate sites and training facilities, speaks before various organizations, and has appeared on radio and television. She has contact with management and with human resources and training departments. Her work schedule has busy and slow periods, but she usually works from 40 to 50 hours a week and sometimes makes evening presentations. She describes her work as exciting, draining, and full of time constraints.

OUTLOOK

The employment of personal appearance workers is expected to grow as fast as the average through 2012, according to the *Occupational Outlook Handbook,* mainly due to increasing population, incomes, and demand for cosmetology services.

Christine Sherlock says the economy has little effect on color consulting. During sluggish times, people still want the lift that such beauty services give them. The demand for consultants is growing steadily, and she believes self-employed people with successful businesses aren't likely to be out of work. The field is evolving, with new opportunities in corporate work.

Susan Fignar says corporate consultants are affected by downsizing because when companies cut personnel they also reduce training. "Right now," she says, "the field is growing." She says the hot topics are casual dress for business, etiquette, communications, and public image. Fignar feels security comes from constantly working to build your consulting business. She advises consultants to develop a 60-second sales pitch so they're always ready to describe their services to any prospective client they meet.

FOR MORE INFORMATION
This organization has information on continuing education, mentorship programs, and certification.
   Association of Image Consultants International
   431 East Locust Street, Suite 300
   Des Moines, IA 50309
   Tel: 515-282-5500
   Email: info@aici.org
   http://www.aici.org

This company provides information on career opportunities in the field. Check out its website for information on their products.
   Color Me Beautiful
   http://www.colormebeautiful.com

———————— INTERVIEW ————————

Marion Gellatly founded Powerful Presence, a California-based image-management training and consulting firm, in 1991. (To learn more about her services, visit http://www.powerful-presence.com.) She is the 2005–2007 President of the Association of Image Consultants International (AICI). AICI is the premier global image organization and represents members in more than 30 countries. Marion is also an executive team member for the Direct Selling Women's Alliance, where she is director of their online Image Center. She was kind enough to discuss her career with the editors of Careers in Focus: Fashion.

Q. Please tell us a little about your business.
A. Powerful Presence's mission is to educate and motivate business people to boost their personal power for effective professional presence, etiquette, and communication. The company does this through workshops, seminars, and individual counseling for men and women. We educate and consult with sectors as varied as high tech, finance, government, hospitality, small and large businesses, and professional associations.

Q. Please briefly describe your primary and secondary job duties.

A. My primary responsibilities are to educate and counsel business professionals on the importance of developing, refining, and maintaining an authentic image that helps them achieve their professional goals. My secondary responsibility is to provide specific image services for the client (i.e., personal shopping, wardrobe development, color analysis, makeup and hair selections, and communication and business etiquette skills).

Q. What are the most important personal and professional qualities for image consultants?

A. The qualities to assure success in this profession are
- integrity
- creativity
- passion for learning and educating
- listening skills
- diplomacy
- solid business skills (marketing and sales, finance, customer service, and technical)
- entrepreneurial spirit

Q. What are some of the pros and cons of your job?

A. Pros

You get to
- be your own boss and set your own pace.
- create your company's vision and mission.
- assist in building a client's confidence and further their professional and personal development.
- promote the profession of image consulting to the world.

Cons
- Start-up costs of the business (technical, marketing, professional development).
- It takes time to build credibility and a client base.
- You must invest in continuing professional development.
- You must be self-motivated to keep your business goals on target.
- You must develop a support system so you don't feel alone in your business.

Q. What advice would you give to students as they look for jobs in this field?

A. • Identify the jobs in this field that you are passionate about and have the talent and interest to pursue. For example, I spent many years in the corporate arena before starting Powerful Presence. Therefore, I knew that the corporate arena would be one that would be a natural fit for me and one in which I had expertise, knowledge, and passion to offer to my target market. For example: if you love the environment of retail, you may find it a natural fit to develop a practice focused on personal shopping and/or wardrobe-development services. Or if you have a highly artistic and creative talent, you may prefer to develop a personal stylist practice and specialize in the celebrity arena.

• The opportunities are vast and allow you to select a segment of the business that fits your talent, expertise, and passion.

• If you are building your own practice, you must stay focused on building your business every hour of every day.

• Prior to starting your own practice, you may consider working with a company or retailer that will provide you with learning experiences that you can use in your business.

• Understand and learn what it takes to run a business. Develop a business plan if you will be self-employed. An image consulting practice cannot be run as a hobby if it is to be profitable. And, business skills are imperative.

Q. What are the benefits of association membership for professionals in this field?

A. The benefits are vast. Belonging to a professional organization like the Association of Image Consultants International (AICI) brings multiple benefits:

• AICI brings together those who require image-consulting services with those who provide those services.

• AICI enhances industry standards through a rigorous three-tiered certification program.

• AICI holds the world's premier annual image-consulting conference.

• AICI provides continuing education classes for image consultants.

• AICI acts as the voice of the image-consulting profession as the media's definitive source for experts on issues and current events that affect or are affected by image consultants.

You may join AICI as a student, associate, or affiliate member. Visit http://www.aici.org for more information and an online application. In addition, AICI brings credibility to its members and offers them networking opportunities with like-minded people. It also provides members with an informal support system of advice and mentoring so members never feel alone.

There are other professional organizations that support the field of image consulting—for example, Fashion Group International and Colour Designers International.

Cosmetologists

QUICK FACTS

School Subjects
Art
Business
Speech

Personal Skills
Artistic
Mechanical/manipulative

Work Environment
Primarily indoors
Primarily one location

Minimum Education Level
Some postsecondary training

Salary Range
$13,100 to $20,500 to $37,140

Certification or Licensing
Required by all states

Outlook
About as fast as the average

DOT
332

GOE
11.04.01

NOC
6271

O*NET-SOC
39-5012.00

OVERVIEW

Cosmetologists practice hair-care skills (including washing, cutting, coloring, perming, and applying various conditioning treatments), esthetics (performing skin care treatments), and nail care (grooming of hands and feet). *Barbers* are not cosmetologists; they undergo separate training and licensing procedures. There are approximately 651,000 cosmetologists, barbers, hairdressers, and hairstylists employed in the United States.

HISTORY

The history of the profession of cosmetology begins with barbering (the Latin *barba* means beard), one of the oldest trades, described by writers in ancient Greece. Relics of rudimentary razors date to the Bronze Age, and drawings of people in early Chinese and Egyptian cultures show men with shaved heads, indicating the existence of a barbering profession.

Barbers often did more than hair care. The treatment of illnesses by bloodletting, a task originally performed by monks, was passed along to barbers in 1163 by the papacy. Although trained physicians were already established at this time, they supported and encouraged the use of barbers for routine medical tasks, such as the treatment of wounds and abscesses. From the 12th century to the 18th century, barbers were known as barber-surgeons. They performed medical and surgical services, such as extracting teeth, treating disease, and cauterizing wounds.

Barbers began to organize and form guilds in the 14th century. A barbers' guild was formed in France in 1361. In 1383, the barber of the king of France was decreed to be the head of that guild.

The Barbers of London was established as a trade guild in 1462. Barbers distinguished themselves from surgeons and physicians by their titles. Barbers, who were trained through apprenticeships, were referred to as doctors of the short robe; university-trained doctors were doctors of the long robe. In England, during the first part of the 16th century, laws were established to limit the medical activities of barbers. They were allowed to let blood and perform tooth extractions only, while surgeons were banned from performing activities relegated to barbers, such as shaving.

Surgeons separated from the barbers' guild in England and in 1800 established their own guild, the Royal College of Surgeons. Laws were passed to restrict the activities of barbers to nonmedical practices. Barbers continued to be trained through apprenticeships until the establishment of barber training schools at the beginning of the 20th century.

Women did not begin to patronize barbershops until the 1920s. The bob, a hairstyle in which women cut their hair just below the ears, became popular at that time. Until that time, women usually wore their hair long. In the 1920s, shorter styles for women became acceptable and women began to go to barbers for cutting and styling. This opened the door for women to join the profession, and many began training to work with women's hairstyles.

Today, women and men patronize hair salons or beauty shops to have their hair cut, styled, and colored. The barber shop, on the other hand, remains largely the domain of men, generally operated by and for men.

Until the 1920s, *beauticians* (as they were commonly known) performed their services in their clients' homes. The beauty salons and shops now so prevalent have emerged as public establishments in more recent years. In the United States—as in many other countries—the cosmetology business is among the largest of the personal service industries.

THE JOB

Cosmetology uses hair as a medium to sculpt, perm, color, or design to create a fashion attitude. Cosmetologists, also known as *hair stylists*, perform all of these tasks as well as provide other services, such as deep conditioning treatments, special-occasion hair designs, and a variety of hair-addition techniques.

A licensed hair stylist can perform the hair services noted above and also is trained and licensed to do the basics of esthetics and nail technology. To specialize in esthetics or nail technology, additional courses are taken in each of these disciplines—or someone can study just esthetics or just nail technology and get a license in either or both of these areas.

Cosmetology schools teach some aspects of human physiology and anatomy, including the bone structure of the head and some elementary facts about the nervous system, in addition to hair skills. Some schools have now added psychology-related courses, dealing with people skills and communications.

Hair stylists may be employed in shops that have as few as one or two employees, or as many as 20 or more. They may work in privately owned salons or in a salon that is part of a large or small chain of beauty shops. They may work in hotels, department stores, hospitals, nursing homes, resort areas, or on cruise ships. In recent years, a number of hair professionals—especially in big cities—have gone to work in larger facilities, sometimes known as spas or institutes, which offer a variety of health and beauty services. One such business, for example, offers complete hair design/treatment/color services; manicures and pedicures; makeup; bridal services; spa services, including different kinds of facials (thermal mask, anti-aging, acne treatment), body treatments (exfoliating sea salt glow, herbal body wrap), scalp treatments, hydrotherapy water treatments, massage therapy, eyebrow/eyelash tweezing and tinting, and hair-removal treatments for all parts of the body; a fashion boutique; and even a wellness center staffed with board-certified physicians.

Those who operate their own shops must also take care of the details of business operations. Bills must be paid, orders placed, invoices and supplies checked, equipment serviced, and records and books kept. The selection, hiring, and termination of other workers are also the owner's responsibility. Like other responsible business people, shop and salon owners are likely to be asked to participate in civic and community projects and activities.

Some stylists work for cosmetic/hair product companies. Sean Woodyard, for instance, in addition to being employed as a stylist at a big-city salon, teaches hair coloring for a major national cosmetics/hair care company. When the company introduces a new product or sells an existing product to a new salon, the company hires hair professionals as "freelance educators" to teach the stylists at the salon how to use the product. Woodyard has traveled all over the country during the past six years, while still keeping his full-time job, teaching color techniques at salons, and also participating in demonstrations for the company at trade shows. "I've taught all levels of classes," he says, "from a very basic color demonstration to a very complex color correction class. I've also been responsible for training other educators. I have really enjoyed traveling to other locales and having the opportunity to see other salons and other parts of the beauty and fashion industry."

At industry shows, what he does has varied. Woodyard is representing the company, "whether I'm standing behind a booth selling products or working on stage, demonstrating the product, or assisting a guest artist backstage, doing preparatory work. This has given me a real hands-on education, and I've been able to work with some of the top hair stylists in the country."

Woodyard has been working, as he says, "behind the chair" for 14 years. His first job after graduating from cosmetology school was at a small barbershop in his hometown. From there, he moved on to a larger salon and then on to work in a big city. "Work behind the chair led me to want to do color," he said. "This really interested me. I guess wanting to know more about it myself is the reason why I researched it and became so involved with color. As I learned more about hair coloring, I became competent and more confident." The challenge, he said, is to learn the "laws of color"—how to choose a shade to get a specific result on a client's hair. He is now considered a color expert and is the head of the chemical department at his salon. "I've always been involved some way in outside education," Woodyard notes. "I've never been in a job where I have just worked 40 hours behind the chair. I've always been involved in some kind of training. I like to share what I know."

Cosmetologists must know how to market themselves to build their business. Whether they are self-employed or work for a salon or company, they are in business for themselves. It is the cosmetologist's skills and personality that will attract or fail to attract clients to that particular cosmetologist's chair. A marketing strategy Woodyard uses is to give several of his business cards to each of his clients. When one of his clients recommends him to a prospective new client, he gives both the old and new client a discount on a hair service.

Karol Thousand is the managing director of corporate school operations for a large cosmetology school that has four campuses in metropolitan areas in two states. She began as a stylist employed by salons and then owned her own shop for seven years. Her business was in an area that was destroyed by a tornado. It was then that she looked at different opportunities to decide the direction of her career. "I looked at the business end of the profession," she said, "and I took some additional business courses and was then introduced to the school aspect of the profession. I have a passion for the beauty business, and as I explored various training programs, I thought to myself, 'Hey, this is something I'd like to do!'"

Karol managed a cosmetology school in Wisconsin before moving to Chicago for her current position. She said, "This is an empowering and satisfying profession. Not only do you make someone look better, but 99 percent of the time, they will feel better about themselves. In cosmetology, you can have the opportunity several times a day to help change the total look and perspective of an individual."

Cosmetologists serving the public must have pleasant, friendly, professional attitudes, as well as skill, ability, and an interest in their craft. These qualities are necessary in building a following of steady customers. The nature of their work requires cosmetologists to be aware of the psychological aspects of dealing with all types of personalities. Sometimes this can require diplomacy skills and a high degree of tolerance in dealing with different clients.

"To me," Sean Woodyard admits, "doing hair is just as much about self-gratification as it is about pleasing the client. It makes me feel good to make somebody else look good and feel good. It's also, of course, a great artistic and creative outlet."

REQUIREMENTS

High School
High school students interested in the cosmetology field can help build a good foundation for postsecondary training by taking subjects in the areas of art, science (especially a basic chemistry course), health, business, and communication arts. Psychology and speech courses could also be helpful.

Postsecondary Training
To become a licensed cosmetologist, you must have completed an undergraduate course of a certain amount of classroom credit hours. The required amount varies from state to state—anywhere from 1,050 to 2,200 hours. The program takes from 10 to 24 months to complete, again depending on the state. Evening courses are also frequently offered, and these take two to four months longer to complete. Applicants must also pass a written test, and some states also give an oral test, before they receive a license. Most states will allow a cosmetologist to work as an apprentice until the license is received, which normally just involves a matter of weeks.

A 1,500-hour undergraduate course at a cosmetology school in Illinois is typical of schools around the country. The program consists of theoretical and practical instruction divided into individual units of learning. Students are taught through the media of theory, audiovisual presentation, lectures, demonstrations, practical hands-on experiences, and written and practical testing. All schools have what they call clinic areas or floors, where people can have their hair done (or avail themselves of esthetics or nail services) by students at a discounted price, compared to what they would pay in a regular shop or salon.

One course, Scientific Approach to Hair Sculpture, teaches students how to sculpt straight and curly hair, ethnic and Caucasian, using shears, texturizing tools and techniques, razors, and electric clippers. Teaching tools include mannequins, slip-ons, hair wefts, rectangles, and profiles. People skills segments are part of each course. Among other courses are Scientific Approach to Perm Design, Systematic Approach to Color, and Systematic Approach to Beauty Care. Three different salon prep courses focus on retailing, business survival skills, and practical applications for contemporary design. The program concludes with final testing, as well as extensive reviews and preparations for state board testing through a mock state board written practical examination.

Karol Thousand noted that, at her school and others throughout the country, "Twenty-five years ago, the courses focused mainly on technical skills. This is still the core focus, but now we teach more interpersonal skills. Our People Skills program helps students understand the individual, the different personality types—to better comprehend how they fit in and how to relate to their clients. We also teach sales and marketing skills—how to sell themselves and their services and products, as well as good business management skills."

Some states offer student internship programs. One such program that was recently initiated in Illinois aims to send better-prepared students/junior stylists into the workforce upon completion of their training from a licensed school. This program allows students to enter into a work-study program for 10 percent of their training in either cosmetology, esthetics, or nail technology. The state requires a student to complete at least 750 hours of training prior to making application for the program.

The program allows a student to experience firsthand the expectations of a salon, to perform salon services to be evaluated by their supervisor, and to experience different types of salon settings. The participating salons have the opportunity to pre-qualify potential employees before they graduate and work with the school regarding the skill levels of the student interns. This will also enhance job placement programs already in place in the school. The state requires that each participating salon be licensed and registered with the appropriate state department and file proof of registration with the school, along with the name and license number of their cosmetologist who is assigned to supervise students, before signing a contract or agreement.

Certification or Licensing
At the completion of the proper amount of credit hours, students must pass a formal examination before they can be licensed. The exam takes just a few hours. Some states also require a practical (hands-on) test and oral exams. Most, however, just require written tests. State board examinations are given at regular intervals. After about a month, test scores are available. Those who have passed then send in a licensure application and a specified fee to the appropriate state department. It takes about four to six weeks for a license to be issued.

Temporary permits are issued in most states, allowing students who have passed the test and applied for a license to practice their profession while they wait to receive the actual license.

Graduate courses on advanced techniques and new methods and styles are also available at many cosmetology schools. Many states require licensed cosmetologists to take a specified number of credit hours, called continuing education units, or CEUs. Licenses must be renewed in all states, generally every year or every two years.

In the majority of states, the minimum age for an individual to obtain a cosmetology license is 16. Because standards and requirements vary from state to state, students are urged to contact the licensing board of the state in which they plan to be employed.

Other Requirements
Hairstyles change from season to season. As a cosmetologist, you will need to keep up with current fashion trends and often be learning new procedures to create new looks. You should be able to visualize different styles and make suggestions to your clients about what is best for them. And even if you don't specialize in coloring hair, you should have a good sense of color. One of your most important responsibilities will be to make your clients feel comfortable around you and happy with their looks. To do this, you will need to develop both your talking and listening skills.

EXPLORING
Talk to friends or parents of friends who are working in the industry, or just go to a local salon or cosmetology school and ask questions about the profession. Go to the library and get books on careers in

the beauty/hair care industry. Search the Internet for related websites. Individuals with an interest in the field might seek after-school or summer employment as a general shop helper in a barbershop or a salon. Some schools may permit potential students to visit and observe classes.

EMPLOYERS

The most common employers of hair stylists are, of course, beauty salons. However, hair stylists also find work at department stores, hospitals, nursing homes, spas, resorts, cruise ships, and cosmetics companies. The demand for services in the cosmetology field—hair styling in particular—far exceeds the supply; additionally, the number of salons increases by 2 percent each year. Considering that most cosmetology schools have placement services to assist graduates, finding employment usually is not difficult for most cosmetologists. As with most jobs in the cosmetology field, opportunities will be concentrated in highly populated areas; however, there will be jobs available for hair stylists virtually everywhere. Many hair stylists/ cosmetologists aspire ultimately to be self-employed. This can be a rewarding avenue if one has plenty of experience and good business sense (not to mention start-up capital or financial backing); it also requires long hours and a great deal of hard work.

STARTING OUT

To be a licensed cosmetologist/hair stylist, you must graduate from an accredited school and pass a state test. Once that is accomplished, you can apply for jobs that are advertised in the newspapers or over the Internet, or apply at an employment agency specializing in these professions. Most schools have placement services to help their graduates find jobs. Some salons have training programs from which they hire new employees.

Scholarships or grants that can help you pay for your schooling are available. One such program is the Access to Cosmetology Education (ACE) Grant. It is sponsored by the American Association of Cosmetology Schools (AACS), the Beauty and Barber Supply Institute Inc., and the Cosmetology Advancement Foundation. Interested students can find out about ACE Grants and obtain applications at participating schools, salons, and distributors or through these institutions. The criteria for receiving an ACE Grant include approval from an AACS member school, recommendations from two salons, and a high school diploma or GED.

ADVANCEMENT

Individuals in the beauty/hair care industry most frequently begin by working at a shop or salon. Many aspire to be self-employed and own their own shop. There are many factors to consider when contemplating going into business on one's own. Usually it is essential to obtain experience and financial capital before seeking to own a shop. The cost of equipping even a one-chair shop can be very high. Owning a large shop or a chain of shops is an aspiration for the very ambitious.

Some pursue advanced educational training in one aspect of beauty culture, such as hair styling or coloring. Others who are more interested in the business aspects can take courses in business management skills and move into shop or salon management, or work for a corporation related to the industry. Manufacturers and distributors frequently have exciting positions available for those with exceptional talent and creativity. Cosmetologists work on the stage as platform artists, or take some additional education courses and teach at a school of cosmetology.

Some schools publish their own texts and other printed materials for students. They want people who have cosmetology knowledge and experience as well as writing skills to write and edit these materials. An artistic director for the publishing venue of one large school has a cosmetology degree in addition to degrees in art. Other cosmetologists might design hairstyles for fashion magazines, industry publications, fashion shows, television presentations, or movies. They might get involved in the regulation of the business, such as working for a state licensing board. There are many and varied career possibilities cosmetologists can explore in the beauty/hair care industry.

EARNINGS

Cosmetologists can make an excellent living in the beauty/hair care industry, but as in most careers, they don't receive very high pay when just starting out. Though their raise in salary may start slowly, the curve quickly escalates. The U.S. Department of Labor reports cosmetologists and hairstylists had a median annual income (including tips) of $20,500 in 2004. The lowest paid 10 percent, which generally included those beginning in the profession, made less than $13,100. The highest paid 10 percent earned more than $37,140. Again, both those salaries include tips. On the extreme upward end of the pay scale, some fashion stylists in New York or Hollywood charge $300 per haircut. Their annual salary can go into six figures.

Salaries in larger cities are greater than those in smaller towns, but the cost of living is higher in big cities, too.

Most shops and salons give a new employee a guaranteed income instead of commission. If the employee goes over the guaranteed amount, then he or she earns a commission. Usually, this guarantee will extend for the first three months of employment, so that the new stylist can focus on building up business before going on straight commission.

In addition, most salon owners grant incentives for product sales; and, of course, there are always tips. However, true professionals never depend on their tips. If a stylist receives a tip, it's a nice surprise for a job well done, but it's good business practice not to expect these bonuses. All tips must be recorded and reported to the Internal Revenue Service.

The benefits a cosmetologist receives, such as health insurance and retirement plans, depend on the place of employment. A small independent salon cannot afford to supply a hefty benefit package, but a large shop or salon or a member of a chain can be more generous. However, some of the professional associations and organizations offer benefit packages at reasonable rates.

WORK ENVIRONMENT

Those employed in the cosmetology industry usually work a five- or six-day week, which averages approximately 40 to 50 hours. Weekends and days preceding holidays may be especially busy. Cosmetologists are on their feet a lot and are usually working in a small space. Strict sanitation codes must be observed in all shops and salons, and they are comfortably heated, ventilated, and well lighted.

Hazards of the trade include nicks and cuts from scissors and razors, minor burns when care is not used in handling hot towels or instruments, and occasional skin irritations arising from constant use of grooming aids that contain chemicals. Some of the chemicals used in hair dyes or permanent solutions can be very abrasive; plastic gloves are required for handling and contact. Pregnant women are advised to avoid contact with many of those chemicals present in hair products.

Conditions vary depending on what environment the stylist is working in. Those employed in department store salons will have more of a guaranteed client flow, with more walk-ins from people who are shopping. A freestanding shop or salon might have a more predictable pace, with more scheduled appointments and fewer walk-ins. In a department store salon, for example, stylists have to abide by the rules and regulations of the store. In a private salon, stylists are more like entrepreneurs or freelancers, but they have much more flexibility as to when they come and go and what type of business they want to do.

Stylist Sean Woodyard said, "I've always enjoyed the atmosphere of a salon. There's constant action and something different happening every day. A salon attracts artistic, creative people and the profession allows me to be part of the fashion industry."

Some may find it difficult to work constantly in such close, personal contact with the public at large, especially when they strive to satisfy customers who are difficult to please or disagreeable. The work demands an even temperament, pleasant disposition, and patience.

OUTLOOK

The future looks good for cosmetology. According to the U.S. Department of Labor, employment should grow about as fast as the average through 2012. Our growing population, the availability of disposable income, and changes in hair fashion that are practically seasonal all contribute to the demand for cosmetologists. In addition, turnover in this career is fairly high as cosmetologists move up into management positions, change careers, or leave the field for other reasons. Competition for jobs at higher paying, prestigious salons, however, is strong.

FOR MORE INFORMATION

Contact the following organization for more information on cosmetology schools and profiles of cosmetologists in the field:

American Association of Cosmetology Schools
15825 North 71st Street, Suite 100
Scottsdale, AZ 85254-1521
Tel: 800-831-1086
http://www.beautyschools.org

Contact the following organization for more information on cosmetology careers:

Beauty and Barber Supply Institute Inc.
15825 North 71st Street, Suite 100
Scottsdale, AZ 85254
Tel: 800-468-2274
Email: info@bbsi.org
http://www.bbsi.org

For information on accredited schools of cosmetology, contact
National Accrediting Commission of Cosmetology Arts and Sciences
4401 Ford Avenue, Suite 1300
Alexandria, VA 22302
Tel: 703-600-7600
http://www.naccas.org

For industry information, contact
National Cosmetology Association
401 North Michigan Avenue, 22nd Floor
Chicago, IL 60611
Tel: 312-527-6765
http://www.salonprofessionals.org

Costume Designers

QUICK FACTS

School Subjects
Art
Family and consumer science
Theater/dance

Personal Skills
Artistic
Following instructions

Work Environment
Primarily indoors
One location with some
    travel

Minimum Education Level
High school diploma

Salary Range
$15,170 to $23,010 to
    $36,780

Certification or Licensing
None available

Outlook
Decline

DOT
346

GOE
01.04.02

NOC
5243

O*NET-SOC
27-1022.00

OVERVIEW

Costume designers plan, create, and maintain clothing and accessories for all characters in a stage, film, television, dance, or opera production. Designers custom fit each character and either create a new garment or alter an existing costume.

HISTORY

Costume design has been an important part of the theater since the early Greek tragedies, when actors generally wore masks and long robes with sleeves. By the time of the Roman Caesars, stage costumes had become very elaborate and colorful.

After the fall of Rome, theater disappeared for some time, but later returned in the form of Easter and Nativity plays. Priests and choirboys wore their usual robes with some simple additions, such as veils and crowns. Plays then moved from the church to the marketplace, and costumes again became important to the production.

During the Renaissance, costumes were designed for the Italian pageants, the French ballets, and the English masques by such famous designers as Torelli, Jean Berain, and Burnacini. From 1760 to 1782, Louis-Rene Boquet designed costumes using wide panniers, forming a kind of elaborate ballet skirt. But by the end of the 18th century, there was a movement toward more classical costumes on the stage.

During the early 19th century, historical costumes became popular, and period details were added to contemporary dress. Toward the end of the 19th century, realism became important, and actors wore the dress of the day, often their own clothes. Because this trend resulted in less work for the costume designers, they turned to musical and opera productions to express their creativity.

In the early 20th century, Diaghilev's Russian Ballet introduced a non-naturalistic style in costumes, most notably in the designs of Leon Bakst. This trend gave way to European avant-garde theater, in which costumes became abstract and symbolic.

Since the 1960s, new materials, such as plastics and adhesives, have greatly increased the costume designer's range. Today, their work is prominent in plays, musicals, dance performances, films, music videos, and television programs.

THE JOB

Costume designers generally work as freelancers. After they have been contracted to provide the costumes for a production, they read the script to learn about the theme, location, time period, character types, dialogue, and action. They meet with the director to discuss his or her feelings on the plot, characters, period and style, time frame for the production, and budget.

For a play, designers plan a rough costume plot, which is a list of costume changes by scene for each character. They thoroughly research the history and setting in which the play is set. They plan a preliminary color scheme and sketch the costumes, including details such as gloves, footwear, hose, purses, jewelry, canes, fans, bouquets, and other props. The costume designer or an assistant collects swatches of fabrics and samples of various accessories.

After completing the research, final color sketches are painted or drawn and mounted for presentation. Once the director approves the designs, the costume designer solicits bids from contractors, creates or rents costumes, and shops for fabrics and accessories. Measurements of all actors are taken. Designers work closely with drapers, sewers, hairstylists, and makeup artists in the costume shop. They supervise fittings and attend all dress rehearsals to make final adjustments and repairs.

Costume designers also work in films, television, and videos, aiming to provide the look that will highlight characters' personalities. Aside from working with actors, they may also design and create costumes for performers such as figure skaters, ballroom dance competitors, circus members, theme park characters, rock artists, and others who routinely wear costumes as part of a show.

REQUIREMENTS

High School

Costume designers need at least a high school education. It is helpful to take classes in art, home economics, and theater and to participate in drama clubs or community theater. English, literature, and history classes will help you learn how to analyze a play and research the clothing and manner of various historical periods. Marketing and business-related classes will also be helpful, as most costume designers work as freelancers. Familiarity with computers is useful, as many designers work with computer-aided design (CAD) programs.

While in high school, consider starting a portfolio of design sketches. Practicing in a sketchbook is a great way to get ideas and

A college design student creates a pattern for a design. *(Corbis)*

designs out on paper and organized for future reference. You can also get design ideas through others; watch theater, television, or movie productions and take note of the characters' dress. Sketch them on your own for practice. Looking through fashion magazines can also give you ideas to sketch.

Postsecondary Training

A college degree is not a requirement, but in this highly competitive field, it gives a sizable advantage. Most costume designers today have a bachelor's degree. Many art schools, especially in New York and Los Angeles, have programs in costume design at both the bachelor's and master's degree level. A liberal arts school with a strong theater program is also a good choice.

Other Requirements

Costume designers need sewing, draping, and patterning skills, as well as training in basic design techniques and figure drawing. Aside from being artistic, designers must also be able to work with people because many compromises and agreements must be made between the designer and the production's director.

Costume designers must prepare a portfolio of their work, including photographs and sketches highlighting their best efforts. Some theatrical organizations require membership in United Scenic Artists (USA), a union that protects the interests of designers on the job and sets minimum fees. Students in design programs that pass an exam and have some design experience can apply for USA's Designer Apprentice Program. More experienced designers who want full professional membership in the union must also submit a portfolio for review.

EXPLORING

If you are interested in costume design, consider joining a theater organization, such as a school drama club or a community theater. School dance troupes or film classes also may offer opportunities to explore costume design.

The Costume Designer's Handbook: A Complete Guide for Amateur and Professional Costume Designers by Rosemary Ingham and Liz Covey (Portsmouth, N.H.: Heinemann, 1992), is an invaluable resource for beginning or experienced costume designers.

You can practice designing on your own, by drawing original sketches or copying designs from television, films, or the stage. Practice sewing and altering costumes from sketches for yourself, friends, and family.

EMPLOYERS

Costume designers are employed by production companies that produce works for stage, television, and film. Most employers are located in New York and Los Angeles, although most metropolitan areas have community theater and film production companies that hire designers.

STARTING OUT

Most high schools and colleges have drama clubs and dance groups that need costumes designed and made. Community theaters, too, may offer opportunities to assist in costume production. Regional theaters hire several hundred costume technicians each year for seasons that last anywhere from 28 to 50 weeks.

Many beginning designers enter the field by becoming an assistant to a designer. Many established designers welcome newcomers and can be generous mentors. Some beginning workers start out in costume shops, which usually requires membership in a union. However, nonunion workers may be allowed to work for short-term projects. Some designers begin as *shoppers*, who swatch fabrics, compare prices, and buy yardage, trim, and accessories. Shoppers learn where to find the best materials at reasonable prices and often establish valuable contacts in the field. Other starting positions include milliner's assistant, craft assistant, or assistant to the draper.

Schools with bachelor's and master's programs in costume design may offer internships that can lead to jobs after graduation. Another method of entering costume design is to contact regional theaters directly and send your resume to the theater's managing director.

Before you become a costume designer, you may want to work as a freelance design assistant for a few years to gain helpful experience, a reputation, contacts, and an impressive portfolio.

ADVANCEMENT

Beginning designers must show they are willing to do a variety of tasks. The theater community is small and intricately interconnected, so those who work hard and are flexible with assignments can gain good reputations quickly. Smaller regional theaters tend to hire designers for a full season to work with the same people on one or more productions, so opportunities for movement may be scarce. Eventually, costume designers with experience and talent can work for larger productions, such as films, television, and videos.

Useful Websites

About.Com: Style/Women's
  Fashion
http://fashion.about.com

Careerthreads.com
http://www.careerthreads.com

E-model.net
http://www.e-model.net

Fashion Club
http://www.fashionclub.com

Fashion Planet
http://www.fashion-planet.com

FashionBook.com
http://www.fashionbook.com

Fashion Era
http://www.fashion-era.com

Fashion-Schools.org
http://www.fashion-schools.org

EARNINGS

Earnings vary greatly in this business depending on factors such as how many outfits the designer completes, how long they are employed during the year, and how much experience they have. Although the U.S. Department of Labor does not give salary figures for costume designers, it does report that the related occupational group of tailors, dressmakers, and custom sewers had a median hourly wage of $11.06 in 2004. For full-time work, this hourly wage translates into a yearly income of approximately $23,010. However, those just starting out and working as assistants earned as little as $7.29 an hour, translating into an annual salary of approximately $15,170. Experienced tailors, dressmakers, and custom sewers earned $17.68 or more per hour (or $36,780 annually).

Costume designers who work on Broadway or for other large stage productions are usually members of the United Scenic Artists union, which sets minimum fees, requires producers to pay into pension and welfare funds, protects the designer's rights, establishes rules for billing, and offers group health and life insurance.

According to the union, a costume designer for a Broadway production with a minimum of 36 actors earned $14,586 in 2005. For opera and dance companies, salary is usually by costume count.

For feature films and television, costume designers earn daily rates for an eight-hour day or a weekly rate for an unlimited number of hours. Designers sometimes earn royalties on their designs.

Regional theaters usually set individual standard fees, which vary widely, beginning around $200 per week for an assistant. Most of them do not require membership in the union.

Most costume designers work freelance and are paid per costume or show. Costume designers can charge $90 to $500 per costume, but some costumes, such as those for figure skaters, can cost thousands of dollars. Freelance costume designers often receive a flat rate for designing costumes for a show. For small and regional theaters, this rate may be in the $400 to $500 range; the flat rate for medium and large productions generally starts at around $1,000. Many costume designers must take second part-time or full-time jobs to supplement their income from costume design.

Freelancers are responsible for their own health insurance, life insurance, and pension plans. They do not receive holiday, sick, or vacation pay.

WORK ENVIRONMENT

Costume designers put in long hours at painstaking detail work. It is a demanding profession that requires flexible, artistic, and practical workers. The schedule can be erratic—a busy period followed by weeks of little or no work. Though costumes are often a crucial part of a production's success, designers usually get little recognition compared to the actors and director.

Designers meet a variety of interesting and gifted people. Every play, film, or concert is different and every production situation is unique, so there is rarely a steady routine. Costume designers must play many roles: artist, sewer, researcher, buyer, manager, and negotiator.

OUTLOOK

The U.S. Department of Labor predicts employment for tailors, dressmakers, and skilled sewers to decline through 2012, and costume designers may not fair much better. The health of the entertainment business, especially theater, is very dependent on the overall economy and public attitudes. Theater budgets and government support for the arts in general have come under pressure in recent years and have limited employment prospects for costume designers. Many theaters, especially small and nonprofit theaters, are cutting their budgets or doing smaller shows that require fewer costumes. Additionally, people are less willing to spend money on tickets or go to theaters during economic downturns or times of crisis.

Nevertheless, opportunities for costume designers exist. As more cable television networks create original programming, demand for costume design in this area is likely to increase. Costume designers are able to work in an increasing number of locations as new regional theaters and cable television companies operate throughout the United States. As a result, however, designers must be willing to travel.

Competition for designer jobs is stiff and will remain so throughout the next decade. The number of qualified costume designers far exceeds the number of jobs available. This is especially true in smaller cities and regions, where there are fewer theaters.

FOR MORE INFORMATION

This union represents costume designers in film and television. For information on the industry and to view costume sketches in an online gallery, contact or check out the following website:

Costume Designers Guild
4730 Woodman Avenue, Suite 430
Sherman Oaks, CA 91423
Tel: 818-905-1557
Email: cdgia@earthlink.net
http://www.costumedesignersguild.com

This organization provides a list of schools, scholarships, and a journal. College memberships are available with opportunities to network among other members who are professionals in the costume field.

Costume Society of America
PO Box 73
Earleville, MD 21919
Tel: 800-272-9447
Email: national.office@costumesocietyamerica.com
http://www.costumesocietyamerica.com

For additional information, contact the following organizations

National Costumers Association
121 North Bosart Avenue
Indianapolis, IN 46201
Tel: 317-351-1940
Email: office@costumers.org
http://www.costumers.org

United States Institute for Theatre Technology
6443 Ridings Road
Syracuse, NY 13206-1111
Tel: 800-938-7488
Email: info@office.usitt.org
http://www.usitt.org

This union represents many costume designers working in New York, Chicago, Los Angeles, Miami, and New England. For information on membership, apprenticeship programs, and other resources on the career, contact

United Scenic Artists Local 829
29 West 38th Street
New York, NY 10018
Tel: 212-581-0300
http://www.usa829.org

Fashion Buyers and Merchandisers

OVERVIEW

Fashion buyers purchase clothing, footwear, and other accessories for retail and wholesale companies. They are usually assigned to a particular specialty such as women's clothing or children's shoes. *Fashion merchandisers* are responsible for the selection, marketing, and advertising of clothing and accessories for retail and wholesale companies. At many companies, the duties of fashion buyers and merchandisers are interchangeable.

HISTORY

The jobs of buyer and merchandiser have been influenced by a variety of historical changes, including the growth of large retail stores in the 20th century. In the past, store owners typically performed almost all of the business activities, including the purchase of merchandise. Large stores, in contrast, had immensely more complicated operations, requiring large numbers of specialized workers, such as sales clerks, receiving and shipping clerks, advertising managers, personnel officers, and buyers. The introduction of mass production systems at factories required more complicated planning, ordering, and scheduling of purchases. A wider range of available merchandise also called for more astute selection and purchasing techniques.

THE JOB

Fashion buyers purchase clothing for retail stores from designers, manufacturers, or wholesalers. They may specialize in a particular

QUICK FACTS

School Subjects
Business
Economics
Mathematics

Personal Skills
Helping/teaching
Leadership/management

Work Environment
Primarily indoors
One location with some travel

Minimum Education Level
High school diploma

Salary Range
$24,380 to $42,230 to $79,340

Certification or Licensing
Voluntary

Outlook
More slowly than the average

DOT
162

GOE
13.02.02

NOC
6233

O*NET-SOC
11-3061.00, 13-1022.00

type of apparel such as women's, men's, or children's clothing or accessories such as handbags, footwear, belts, or jewelry. Buyers employed at larger department stores may specialize further within a department, say women's denim or men's knitwear.

Fashion buyers, armed with a budget set by retail headquarters, develop a buying plan that meets the needs of their store and its customers. Buyers take into account their store's reputation and goals. For example, overly trendy or flashy pieces probably would not sell well at a store that caters to conservative customers. Most importantly, buyers listen to the opinions of loyal store customers and what styles they enjoy wearing and clothing lines they look for when shopping. After all, a happy customer signals a job well done.

Fashion merchandisers are responsible for purchasing clothing lines to be sold in retail stores, as well as in wholesale settings. Some merchandisers are assigned to oversee the inventory of one store, though it is not uncommon for merchandisers to be responsible for the inventories of all the stores in a nationwide chain. Merchandisers identify and purchase styles and pieces that they feel will appeal to the customer base. They work with store marketing departments in making choices of when and how such inventory should be purchased and distributed to stores. At times, they work directly with designers to turn ideas into actual fashion pieces. They also maintain contacts with different fashion designers, suppliers, and vendors throughout the world. Travel to different countries is often necessary to inspect designs, fabrics, threads, and other embellishments up close—though more and more of such consultations are done via the Internet.

At some companies, fashion buyers share merchandising duties. In fact, many of the responsibilities of buyers and merchandisers are interchangeable, depending on their place of employment, especially at smaller stores. Both fashion buyers and merchandisers keep up with the current trends by studying market reports, attending endless fashion shows, talking with industry consultants, and finding the latest up and coming designers. They have knowledge of different fabrics, textiles, and knitted patterns, and how they look paired with one another. They must also be aware of such details as cost, durability, and cleaning concerns. Merchandisers and buyers, depending on their area of specialty, work with multiple seasonal deadlines. Turnaround time is often lengthy—it takes time to design, sew, and finish clothing pieces—so merchandisers and buyers very often work two or three seasons ahead of what is currently shown in stores.

Once an order is placed, merchandisers and buyers ensure a fair price for the items, and set up a delivery timetable. Upon delivery they check order invoices, and oversee the distribution of merchandise to different stores to ensure adequate stock levels.

Merchandisers and buyers also have a say in how new merchandise is to be displayed in the stores. They often work with advertising and marketing departments in planning decor, signage, lighting, and fixtures such as stands, shelving, and mannequins. They also work alongside stylists in piecing outfits together for display, and adding different accessories to complete a new look. They may work on the creation and updating of store websites and print advertising materials. Buyers and merchandisers may also be called upon to explain the season's new themes and colors to store managers and sales staff, giving them better knowledge of the merchandise.

REQUIREMENTS

High School
A high school diploma generally is required for entering this field. Useful high school courses include mathematics, business, English, and economics. If your high school offers any fashion-related classes, be sure to take them.

Postsecondary Training
A college degree may not be a requirement for becoming a buyer or merchandiser, but it is becoming increasingly important, especially for advancement. A majority of buyers and merchandisers have attended college, many majoring in fashion merchandising, marketing, advertising, purchasing, or business. Joanna attended the Fashion Institute of Technology in New York City and graduated with a bachelor's degree in fashion merchandising management. Regardless of the major, useful courses in preparation for a career in buying/merchandising include accounting, economics, commercial law, finance, advertising, marketing, and various business classes, such as business communications, business organization and management, and computer applications in business.

Retailing experience is helpful to gain a sense of customer tastes and witness the supply and demand process. Additional training is available through trade associations, such as the National Association of Purchasing Management, which sponsors conferences, seminars, and workshops.

Certification or Licensing
Certification, although not required, is becoming increasingly important. Various levels of certification are available through the

American Purchasing Society and the National Association of Purchasing Management. To earn most certifications you must have work experience, meet education requirements, and pass written and oral exams.

Other Requirements
If you are interested in becoming a buyer, you should be organized and have excellent decision-making skills. Predicting consumer tastes and keeping stores and wholesalers appropriately stocked requires resourcefulness, good judgment, and confidence. You should also have skills in marketing to identify and promote products that will sell. Finally, leadership skills are needed to supervise assistant buyers and deal with manufacturers' representatives and store executives.

EXPLORING

One way to explore the retailing field is through part-time or summer employment in a store. A good time to look for such work is during the Christmas holiday season. Door-to-door selling is another way to gain business retailing experience. Occasionally, experience in a retail store can be found through special high school programs.

EMPLOYERS

Buyers and merchandisers work for a wide variety of businesses, both wholesale and retail. Employers range from small stores, where buying and merchandising may be only one function of a manager's job, to multinational corporations, where a buyer or merchandiser may specialize in one type of item.

STARTING OUT

Most buyers find their first job by applying to the personnel office of a retail establishment or wholesaler. Because knowledge of retailing is important, buyers may be required to have work experience in a store.

Most buyers and merchandisers begin their careers as retail sales workers. The next step may be *head of stock*. The head of stock maintains stock inventory records and keeps the merchandise in a neat and well-organized fashion both to protect its value and to permit easy access. He or she usually supervises the work of several employees. This person also works in an intermediate position between the salespeople on the floor and the buyer who provides the merchandise. The next step to becoming a buyer or merchandiser may be assistant buyer or assistant merchandiser. For many department stores, promotion to full buyer or merchandiser requires this background.

Large department stores or chains operate executive training programs for college graduates who seek buying and other retail executive positions. A typical program consists of 16 successive weeks of work in a variety of departments. This on-the-job experience is supplemented by formal classroom work that most often is conducted by senior executives and training department personnel. Following this orientation, trainees are placed in junior management positions for an additional period of supervised experience and training.

ADVANCEMENT

Buyers and merchandisers are key employees of the stores or companies that employ them. One way they advance is through increased responsibility, such as more authority to make commitments for merchandise and more complicated buying assignments.

Buyers and merchandisers are sometimes promoted to *merchandise manager,* which requires them to supervise other buyers and merchandisers, help develop the store's purchasing or merchandising policies, and coordinate buying and selling activities with related departments. Some merchandise managers go on to supervise entire divisions—that is the career path that Joanna would eventually like to take. Other buyers and merchandisers may become vice presidents in charge of purchasing or merchandising or even store presidents. Because buyers and merchandisers learn much about retailing in their job, they are in a position to advance to top executive positions. Some buyers and merchandisers use their knowledge of retailing and the contacts they have developed with suppliers to set up their own businesses.

EARNINGS

How much a buyer earns depends on various factors, including the employer's sales volume. Mass merchandisers, such as discount or chain department stores, pay among the highest salaries.

The U.S. Department of Labor reports the median annual income for buyers was $42,230 in 2004. The lowest paid 10 percent of these buyers made less than $24,380 yearly, and at the other end of the pay range, the highest paid 10 percent earned more than $79,340 annually.

Most buyers and merchandisers receive the usual benefits, such as vacation, sick leave, life and health insurance, and pension plans.

Retail buyers and merchandisers may receive cash bonuses for their work and may also receive discounts on merchandise they purchase from their employer.

WORK ENVIRONMENT

Buyers work in a dynamic and sometimes stressful atmosphere. They must make important decisions on an hourly basis. The results of their work, both successes and failures, show up quickly on the profit and loss statement.

Buyers frequently work long or irregular hours. Evening and weekend hours are common, especially during the holiday season, when the retail field is at its busiest. Extra hours may be required to bring records up to date, for example, or to review stock and to become familiar with the store's overall marketing design for the coming season. Travel may also be a regular part of a buyer's job, possibly requiring several days away from home each month.

Although buyers must sometimes work under pressure, they usually work in pleasant, well-lit environments. They also benefit from having a diverse set of responsibilities.

OUTLOOK

According to the U.S. Department of Labor, employment of buyers and merchandisers in all industries is projected to grow more slowly than the average through 2012. Reasons for this decrease include the large number of business mergers and acquisitions, which results in the blending of buying and merchandising departments and the elimination of redundant jobs. In addition, the use of computers, which increases efficiency, and the trend of some large retail companies to centralize their operations will both contribute to fewer new jobs for buyers and merchandisers. Some job openings will result from the need to hire replacement workers for those who leave the field. Employment prospects should be better for fashion buyers and merchandisers as the industry as a whole continues to enjoy steady growth.

FOR MORE INFORMATION

For career information and job listings, contact
  American Purchasing Society
  PO Box 256
  Aurora, IL 60506

Tel: 630-859-0250
http://www.american-purchasing.com

For information on the magazine Your Future Purchasing Career, *lists of colleges with purchasing programs, and interviews with people in the field, contact the ISM:*
Institute for Supply Management (ISM)
PO Box 22160
Tempe, AZ 85285-2160
Tel: 800-888-6276
http://www.ism.ws

For materials on educational programs in the retail industry, contact
National Retail Federation
325 7th Street, NW, Suite 1100
Washington, DC 20004
Tel: 800-673-4692
http://www.nrf.com

For career information, visit the following website
Career Threads
http://careerthreads.com

Fashion Coordinators

QUICK FACTS

School Subjects
Business
English

Personal Skills
Communication/ideas
Leadership/management

Work Environment
Primarily indoors
One location with some
travel

Minimum Education Level
Bachelor's degree

Salary Range
$25,000 to $37,000 to
$100,000+

Certification or Licensing
None available

Outlook
About as fast as the average

DOT
N/A

GOE
N/A

NOC
N/A

O*NET-SOC
N/A

OVERVIEW

Fashion coordinators are responsible for producing fashion shows and other promotional vehicles for companies and designers. Some are responsible for a particular department, for example, men's apparel, while others may be responsible for the promotion of the entire apparel and accessories line. The majority of these workers are employed by design firms, retail corporations, and apparel centers. Some fashion coordinators work in the entertainment industry.

HISTORY

During the 1970s and 1980s, the fashion industry was revolutionized by the increasing popularity of ready-to-wear fashions. Major designers began to show lines of clothing intended for the average consumer. This move from producing only haute couture to making more affordable—and wearable—clothing gave the middle class access to the latest fashions.

The public's interest in fashion has also been fueled by the growing importance of fashion in other fields, especially media and entertainment. The careers of stylists and fashion coordinators came from the need to design and advise on the use of fashion in advertising campaigns in print, television, and live formats. Also, the entertainment industry needed fashion experts to help coordinate clothing and accessories for actors, actresses, and musicians. The coordinator working in the entertainment world needs to be aware of the setting (stage, backdrops, lighting) in which the actor, actress, or musician will appear. The fashion coordinator must also use management and office skills to arrange schedules, select locations for shows, and keep records and do billing.

THE JOB

Fashion coordinators, whether employed by retail giants, design firms, or shopping centers, are responsible for promoting fashion trends. The main way to promote fashion is through a fashion show. Depending on the size of the company, coordinators may be responsible for a monthly show or for as many as 50 shows or more a year.

There are different types of fashion shows. Vendor or designer shows arrive at the coordinator's office almost pre-packaged. The outfits are already accessorized and are boxed in the order in which the clothes should be shown. Little preparation is needed to produce this show, aside from booking models and setting up a stage. In addition to what fashions are shown, the designer is also in charge of the commentary and backdrops. Vendor shows typically take only a few days to produce. The designer or design firm owns the rights to these fashion shows. Many vendor-type fashion shows take place within the department's sales floor so the public can shop for the clothes as soon as the show ends.

Trend shows are owned by the retailer and are produced by the fashion coordinator and his or her staff. With these shows, coordinators are responsible for putting together outfits and accessories, choosing the choreography and staging, and most importantly, deciding on the message. Every show sends a particular message, or theme, to the audience. For example, what will be important in fashion for the next season? Leather? Wool? Fur? Trend shows are usually produced two or three times a year and scheduled to coincide with the upcoming season. (However, fashions are spotlighted one or two seasons ahead of the calendar year. For example, spring/summer fashions will be shown in the fall/winter months.) It often takes a few weeks or a month to put together a trend show.

Trend shows have important public relations value. Oftentimes a sponsor will give additional support to help a retail store in the show's production. Tickets to the show may be sold to the public, and proceeds from the fashion show may be donated to charity. This not only helps promote upcoming fashion lines, but it also highlights the store's interest in supporting worthy causes and provides the sponsor with publicity.

There are several steps to producing a show, regardless of the scale of the production. First, a budget is set. Then models must be cast to fit the type of clothes. Sometimes as many as 300 models are auditioned before the coordinator selects the final 30 or so to work the trend show. Coordinators often use trusted *modeling agents* to find the best men, women, or children. *Stylists* are used to give the models and their clothes a finished look. *Hairdressers, makeup artists,* and *dressers* prepare the models before the show and during outfit changes. *Production workers* are responsible for finding the right music and lighting. The fashion coordinator and assistants are also responsible for the promotion and execution of a fashion show. They send invitations to the public and media and prepare advertising, as well as set up chairs and props and check on other last minute details.

The fashion coordinator is also responsible for producing fashion shows at other locations besides one retail store. Travel is a large part of this job. Besides traveling to other store locations, fashion coordinators often travel to meet with designers, many of whom are headquartered in New York. Meeting with famous designers may be intimidating at first, but as the coordinator gains experience these meetings can become less nerve racking.

Another important part of a fashion coordinator's job is to help with promotion of a store's fashion lines through television or newspaper and magazine spreads. Oftentimes, local television stations, newspapers, or fashion magazines will request the use of clothing from a store for a particular segment. For example, the TV station may need an outfit for the evening news anchor or the paper may need an outfit for a model in a travel section. The fashion coordinator pulls the appropriate clothing from the sales floor—be it a business suit or cruise wear—then coordinates the outfits with shoes and other accessories and delivers the chosen items to the TV station, newspaper, or magazine offices. After the clothes are returned, the fashion coordinator and his or her staff are responsible for taking the items back to the sales floor and returning them to the racks. The store is given credit by the television station or publication in return for the use of the clothes.

The fashion coordinator's office is part of the marketing side of the fashion industry. Coordinators work alongside *trend forecasters, product developers,* and *planners* in promoting current fashion trends, as well as predicting what the public will desire in fashion for the future.

REQUIREMENTS

High School

High school classes that are fashion related can help acquaint you with the industry. Some schools, such as the High School of Fashion Industries (http://fashionhighschool.net) in New York City, offer fashion-related courses such as fashion design, illustration, fashion merchandising, and art and art history, along with the more traditional academic classes. Even if your high school does not offer specialized fashion courses, you can still prepare for this work by taking classes such as family and consumer science. Take art classes to learn about color and composition. English and speech classes will help you develop the communication skills essential for this line of work. You may be surprised to find out that a knowledge of math is useful in this field, so don't neglect mathematics courses. You may also want to take business or accounting classes since many fashion coordinators are responsible for accounting and budgeting for fashion shows.

Postsecondary Training

While college education may not be absolutely necessary for every fashion job, in this case, a bachelor's degree plus experience will give you an edge over the candidate working solely on past job skills. Most fashion coordinators have degrees in fashion design and merchandising, marketing, or other business-related courses. Computer skills are also important. Many companies rely on computer-aided design software to complete many projects.

It's imperative to spend time in an internship, preferably with a company you hope to be employed by after graduation. Companies prefer to hire graduates who have relevant work experience. In fact, many companies offer their interns full-time positions. If you are unable to find an internship in the fashion industry, consider internships in the music and entertainment industries. These fields are also important sources of fashion trends. Internships at popular entertainment houses such as MTV or VH1 will give you the opportunity to see the role fashion plays in promoting an image as well as give you work experience.

Other Requirements

Fashion coordinators must be hard-working, organized, and well-rounded individuals. They often juggle many tasks simultaneously in order to meet deadlines or produce a flawless fashion show. Be prepared to mingle with the high-power fashion elite one minute and set up folding chairs the next.

A strong sense of fashion is important. You should have an eye for color, design, and what is fashionable. Fashion sense can be learned, but the interest must be present before it can be nurtured. Fashion coordinators, along with anyone working in the fashion industry, keep current by reading fashion magazines and newspapers and visiting websites devoted to fashion.

EXPLORING

Consider being a volunteer at fashion shows, especially those at the local level. Many such productions have smaller budgets, so volunteers are always welcome. No matter what the task, whether helping models with outfit changes, setting up chairs, or passing out brochures, you will get valuable hands-on experience. Take the time to talk to people producing the show and in the show. Ask them about their work and training. You can also make contacts at modeling conventions.

Apply for internships in the fashion industry. Don't forget to make valuable contacts while you are there. Ask questions, and watch those you would like to emulate.

You could also produce a fashion show in your high school to explore this line of work. Your models can be fellow classmates; clothing and accessories can be borrowed from the local mall. Adopt a theme that would interest your peers, say, fashions for the prom or the latest in summer swimwear.

Get experience as a coordinator and producer by putting together a calendar featuring a particular high school group. Pick a theme that is interesting and challenging, such as spotlighting an athletic team, drama club members, or even favorite teachers. Clothes can be borrowed locally, and photography, production, and promotion can be done in-house.

EMPLOYERS

Fashion coordinators are employed by retail corporations, fashion companies, and apparel centers. The fashion capitals of New York City, Milan, London, and Los Angeles, of course, will have plenty of employment opportunities, but those who want to enter this business should be ready to face fierce competition. The fashion industry is very tight-knit, and industry contacts are often the best source of jobs. Employment can be found in other areas of the United States, especially large metropolitan areas. However, according to Pam Zuckerman, career counselor from the Fashion Institute of Technology in New York, "if you want a fashion career in Timbuktu, it's not going to happen. You have to go where the fashion [industry] is."

STARTING OUT

Pam Zuckerman warns that the job of fashion coordinator is not an entry-level position. While being a fashion coordinator may sound like fun, it's a top-level position that is difficult to reach. She notes many young people want to be fashion coordinators. Frequently, however, they don't realize what training and dedication are needed for this job.

A common career path to take would be to begin as a *stylist*—a person who puts together a particular look for other people through choices in clothing, hair, makeup, and accessories. Some successful fashion coordinators have also climbed the corporate ladder working as assistants to coordinators, fashion directors, or fashion designers. Paying your dues in a lower-level position is important, since many companies like to promote from within the department.

ADVANCEMENT

The fashion coordinator position is considered a high rung in the fashion industry ladder. One advancement possibility for a fashion coordinator would be to move deeper into the marketing side of the fashion industry by working as a product developer or fashion forecaster. *Product developers* produce in-house lines of apparel and accessories. *Fashion forecasters,* using a variety of tools, such as surveys, current styles, and market research, try to predict future trends in fashion.

Another way to advance in this career is by transferring to a larger company or design firm, which usually means more responsibilities and a higher salary.

EARNINGS

There are no formal salary surveys available for this particular career. However, according to industry experts, most salaried stylists should expect to earn from $25,000 to $37,000 annually. Stylists working on a freelance basis can also earn as much, though they are paid only after a project is completed as opposed to weekly or bimonthly. Some successful fashion coordinators, especially those employed by larger corporations or well-known design houses, can earn more than $100,000 a year.

Salaried fashion coordinators and stylists usually receive benefits such as heath insurance, paid vacation and sick time, and retirement plans. Some companies may also offer employee discounts.

WORK ENVIRONMENT

Most fashion coordinators work in comfortable, well-lit offices. However, their duties also take them outside of the office. Many times, coordinators must go to different departments or boutiques to choose clothing and accessories for a show from various fashion lines. They often travel to other cities and countries to meet with designers, attend shows, or visit other store locations. Fashion coordinators work 40 hours a week, though it is not unusual to work a lot of overtime, especially when a fashion show is scheduled. Weekend work is expected so that deadlines can be met.

This job, like most in the industry, is in a creative and artistic atmosphere. Fashion coordinators should be prepared to work with a diverse group of people, such as designers, models, stylists, and CEOs. They should be able to deal with different types of personalities and varying sizes of ego.

OUTLOOK

Employment in this career should be good for the next decade. Many opportunities will occur as a result of the creation of new positions in the field or current employees retiring or leaving the workforce for other reasons. Most jobs in the United States will be available in densely populated areas, especially New York City, Chicago, Los Angeles, and Miami.

As fashion trends change, so too must the way runway shows are presented. Themes reflect the taste of the fashion consumer—flashy styles translate to loud, heavily choreographed shows; understated clothing may call for softer presentations. One style of show, as seen by a popular Chicago fashion show producer, has no spoken commentary. Instead, messages in words and images are shown on the backdrop. More recently, the company Victoria's Secret produced revolutionary shows that were accessible on the Internet (and were later broadcast on television). By logging on to the company's website, the public had a live front-row view to the latest in lingerie fashions. These new and varied types of shows should provide employment opportunities for the creative and hip fashion coordinator.

FOR MORE INFORMATION

For information on the industry, student membership, or networking opportunities, contact
   Fashion Group International Inc.
   8 West 40th Street, 7th Floor
   New York, NY 10018
   Tel: 212-302-5511
   Email: info@fgi.org
   http://www.fgi.org

To learn more about the programs and exhibitions offered at FIT, visit its website or contact
Fashion Institute of Technology (FIT)
Seventh Avenue at 27th Street
New York, NY 10001-5992
Tel: 212-217-7999
Email: FITinfo@fitsuny.edu
http://www.fitnyc.edu

One of the degrees offered at this school is in fashion marketing and management. For information on admissions and to view sample student portfolios, visit its website.
Illinois Institute of Art at Chicago
350 North Orleans Street
Chicago, IL 60654
Tel: 800-351-3450
http://www.ilia.aii.edu

7th on Sixth offers venues for designers to showcase their latest fashions. For volunteer opportunities, contact
7th on Sixth
IMG
22 East 71st Street
New York, NY 10021
Tel: 212-253-2692
Email: info@7thonsixth.com
http://www.7thonsixth.com

For career information, visit the following website:
Career Threads
http://careerthreads.com

For subscription information, contact
Women's Wear Daily
http://www.wwd.com

Fashion Designers

QUICK FACTS

School Subjects
Art
Family and consumer science

Personal Skills
Artistic
Communication/ideas

Work Environment
Primarily indoors
One location with some travel

Minimum Education Level
Some postsecondary training

Salary Range
$27,970 to $55,840 to
$150,000+

Certification or Licensing
None available

Outlook
About as fast as the average

DOT
141

GOE
01.04.02

NOC
5243

O*NET-SOC
27-1022.00

OVERVIEW

Fashion designers create or adapt original designs for clothing for men, women, and children. Most specialize in one particular type of clothing, such as women's dresses or men's suits. Most designers work for textile, apparel, and pattern manufacturers. Some designers are self-employed and develop a clientele of individual customers or manufacturers. Others work for fashion salons, high-fashion department stores, and specialty shops. A few work in the entertainment industry, designing costumes. There are approximately 15,000 fashion designers employed in the United States.

HISTORY

Originally, people wore garments to help them maintain body temperature rather than for style. Clothing usually was handmade at home. Dress design became a profession around the 1600s. Before the invention of the sewing machine in 1846 by Elias Howe, all garments were made by hand. One of the first designers was Rose Bertin, a French milliner (creator of fashion accessories such as hats and cloaks) who dressed Marie Antoinette and influenced women's fashions before and during the French Revolution.

Women dominated dress design until 1858, when Charles Frederick Worth, an English tailor and couturier of Empress Eugenie, consort of Napoleon III, opened a salon, or fashion house, in Paris. There, he produced designs for actresses and other wealthy clients—the only individuals with enough time and money to have clothing created specifically for them. Worth was the first designer to make garments from fabrics he had selected; until that time, dressmakers had used fabrics provided by patrons. Worth also was the first designer to display his creations on live models. Today, French designers continue to dominate the field. However, the U.S. garment industry has assumed a position of leadership in clothing design and production in the last 40 years, as London and Milan also have become important fashion centers.

THE JOB

Fashion designers create designs for almost anything that is a part of the costume of men, women, or children. They design both outer and inner garments, hats, purses, shoes, gloves, costume jewelry, scarves, or beachwear. Some specialize in certain types of clothing, such as bridal gowns or sportswear. People in this profession range from the few top haute couture designers who produce one-of-a-kind designs for high-fashion houses, to the thousands of designers who create fashions for mass production and sale to millions of Americans. The largest number of fashion designers are followers rather than originators of fashion, adapting high-end styles to meet the desires of the general public. Many fashion designers are self-employed; some work on a freelance basis.

The designer's original idea for a garment is usually sketched. After a rough sketch is created, the designer begins to shape the pattern pieces that make the garment. The pieces are drawn to actual size on paper and cut out of a rough material, often muslin. The muslin pieces are sewn together and fitted on a model. The designer makes modifications in the pattern pieces or other features of the rough mock-up to complete the design. From the rough model, sample garments are made in the fabric that the designer intends to use.

Today's designers are greatly assisted by computer software. Computer-aided designing and computer-aided manufacturing allow for thousands of fashion styles and colors to be stored in a computer and accessed at the touch of a button, largely eliminating the long process of gathering fabrics and styling them into samples.

Sample garments are displayed at a "showing," to which *press representatives* and *buyers* are invited to see the latest designs. Major designers may present large runway shows twice a year to leading retailers and the fashion press for potential publicity and sales. Sample garments may then be mass-produced, displayed by *fashion models,* and shipped to stores where they are available for purchase.

In some companies, designers are involved in every step of the production of a selected line, from the original idea to the completed garments. Many designers prefer to supervise their own workrooms.

Others work with supervisors to solve problems that arise in the production of the garments.

Most manufacturers produce new styles four times each year: spring and summer; fall and winter; vacation wear; and holiday styles. Designers generally are expected to create between 50 and 150 styles for each showing. Their work calendar differs from the actual time of year. They must be working on spring and summer designs during fall and winter, and on fall and winter clothing during the summer, so as to prepare for a future season's fashion production.

Designers work cooperatively with the head of their manufacturing firm. They design a line that is consistent with the ideas of their employers. They also work cooperatively with those who do the actual production of the garments and must be able to estimate the cost of a garment. Some company designers produce designs and oversee a workroom staff, which may consist of a head designer, an assistant designer, and one or more sample makers. Designers in large firms may plan and direct the work of one or more assistant designers, select fabrics and trims, and help determine the pricing of the products they design.

Designers spend time in exploration and research, visiting textile manufacturing and sales establishments to learn of the latest fabrics and their uses and capabilities. They must know about fabric, weave, draping qualities, and strength of materials. A good understanding of textiles and their qualities underlies much of designers' work. They browse through stores to see what fashion items the public buy and which are passed by. They visit museums and art galleries to get ideas about color and design. They go to places where people congregate—theaters, sports events, business and professional meetings, and resorts—and meet with marketing and production workers, salespeople, and clients to discover what people are wearing and to discuss ideas and styles.

Designers also keep abreast of changing styles. If the styles are too different from public taste, customers will probably reject the designs. If, however, they cling to styles that have been successful in the past, they may find that the taste of buyers has changed dramatically. In either case, it could be equally disastrous for their employers.

There are many opportunities for specialization in fashion design. The most common specialties are particular types of garments such as resort wear, bridalwear, or sportswear.

An interesting specialty in fashion design is theatrical design, a relatively limited field but challenging to those who are interested in combining an interest in theater with a talent for clothing design.

Two fashion designers discuss the fabric they will use for a design. *(Corbis)*

REQUIREMENTS

High School
A high school diploma is needed for fashion designing and should include courses that prepare you for more specialized training after graduation. Art, home economics, mathematics, and chemistry should all be included.

Postsecondary Training
An aspiring designer with a total fashion background that includes marketing and other business skills will be favored by employers over a talented person with no knowledge of business procedures. A college degree is recommended, although not required. Graduation from a fashion design school is highly desirable. Employers seek designers who have had courses in mathematics, business, design, sketching, art history, costume history, literature, pattern making, clothing construction, and textiles.

Some colleges offer a four-year degree in fine arts with a major in fashion design. Many reputable schools of fashion design offer a two- or three-year program that offers a diploma or certificate.

Students interested in fashion should take computer-aided design courses, as computers are increasingly being used by designers to better visualize a final product, create prototypes, and reduce design production time and cost. Companies are looking for more than design skills, many require extensive knowledge and experience with software programs used to produce technical drawings.

Other Requirements

Prospective fashion designers must be artistic and imaginative with a flair for color and clothing coordination. They will need a working knowledge of clothing construction and an eye for trends. They must possess technical aptitudes, problem-solving skills, and the ability to conceptualize in two and three dimensions. Personal qualifications include self-motivation, team spirit, and the ability to handle pressure, deadlines, and long hours. This career also demands energy and a good head for business.

EXPLORING

If you enjoy sewing, you may have taken the first step toward exploring a career in the fashion world. If your skills in garment construction are adequate, the next step may be an attempt at designing and making clothing. Art and design courses will help assess your talent and ability as a creative artist.

If you are able to obtain a summer job in a department or specialty store, you can observe retailing practices and gain some practical insights into the merchandising aspects of the fashion world. Working in a fabric store can provide the opportunity to learn about fabrics and accessories. You may want to visit a garment manufacturer to see fashion employees at work.

You also can attend style shows, visit art galleries, observe clothing worn by fashion leaders, and browse through a variety of stores in which garments are sold. Many useful books and magazines are published about fashion. The so-called fashion industry bible is *Women's Wear Daily,* a must-read for those who want to be knowledgeable and current in this fast-changing business. For subscription information, visit http://www.wwd.com.

EMPLOYERS

Many fashion designers find employment with large fashion houses such as Liz Claiborne or Jones New York. Some large manufacturers produce a secondary line of lower-priced designer clothing—Donna Karan's DKNY and Giorgio Armani's Emporio, for example. In the United States, New York City, San Francisco, and Los Angeles are major fashion centers and positions may be found in both large and small companies. Work also may be found in Chicago and other cities, although not as many jobs are available in these locations.

A few fashion designers work for high-fashion firms, but these positions are difficult to come by and competition is very strong. An aspiring designer may have more options in specialized areas of fashion such as sportswear, sleepwear, children's clothing, or accessories.

Other areas for aspiring fashion designers to explore are home fashions such as bed and bath linens, draperies, and rugs or carpeting. Positions also can be found with pattern manufacturers. Some fashion designers work on a freelance basis, contracting with manufacturers or individuals.

An easy way to learn about manufacturers is to visit a department or specialty store and examine labels and tags on merchandise of interest. In addition to major department stores, retailers such as Target carry a variety of manufacturers' lines.

STARTING OUT

Few people begin their careers as fashion designers. Well-trained college graduates often begin as *assistant designers*. Assistants must prove their ability before being entrusted with the responsible job of the designer. Many young people find that assistant designer jobs are difficult to locate, so they accept beginning jobs in the workroom where they spend time cutting or constructing garments.

Fashion design school graduates may receive placement information from their school or college career services offices. Approaching stores and manufacturers directly is another way to secure a beginning position. However, you will be more successful if you have contacts in the industry through previous summer or part-time work.

ADVANCEMENT

Advancement in fashion designing varies a great deal. There is much moving from firm to firm, and vacancies occur frequently. Aspiring designers should create, collect, and continuously update their portfolios of designs and look for opportunities to show their work to employers. Beginners may work as cutting assistants or assistant designers. From these entry-level positions, the fashion designer's career path may lead to positions as an assistant technical designer, pattern company designer, designer, and head designer. Those who grow with a company may design less and take on more operational responsibilities.

Designers may choose to move into a business or merchandising position where they direct lines, set prices, supervise production, and work directly with buyers. After years of work, top designers may become partners in the design or apparel firms for which they work. Others may open their own retail clothing stores. A designer may want to work for firms that offer increasing design responsibility and fewer restrictions to become established as a house designer or eventually as an independent-name designer.

EARNINGS

Fashion designers earned an average annual salary of $55,840 in 2004, according to the U.S. Department of Labor. The lowest paid 10 percent earned less than $27,970; the highest paid 10 percent earned more than $112,840. A few highly skilled and well-known designers in top firms have annual incomes of more than $150,000. Top fashion designers who have successful lines of clothing can earn bonuses that bring their annual incomes into the millions. As designers become well known, they are usually offered a share of the ownership of the company for which they design. Their ownership percentage increases with their reputation.

Theatrical designers usually work on a contract basis. Although the compensation for the total contract is usually good, there may be long periods of idleness between contracts. The annual incomes for theatrical designers usually are not as great as those of fashion designers, although while they are working they may make more than $1,000 per week.

WORK ENVIRONMENT

Fashion design is competitive and stressful, but often exciting and glamorous. Many designers work in cluttered and noisy surroundings. Their work environment may consist of a large room with long tables for cutting out patterns or garments. There may be only one or two other people working in the room, or there may be several other workers. Many designers travel a great deal for showings and conferences. They may spend time in stores or shops looking at clothing that has been manufactured by competitors.

Most designers work a 40-hour week, but they may have to work more during rush periods. Styles previewed for one season require a great amount of work during the weeks and months before a show. The work pace is usually hectic as pressure builds before collection showings.

OUTLOOK

Designers are key people in the garment industry, yet relatively few of them are needed to make employment possible for thousands of people in other apparel occupations. It is estimated that there are approximately 15,000 fashion designers in the United States, which represents less than 1 percent of the garment industry. Some designers work only for the high-priced custom trade, some for the mass market, and some on exclusive designs that will be made for only one person. Many designers are employed by manufacturers of paper patterns.

Good designers will always be needed, although not in great numbers. However, increasing populations and growing personal incomes are expected to spur the demand for fashion designers. According to the *Occupational Outlook Handbook,* employment of designers is expected to grow about as fast as the average for all occupations through 2012.

Some fashion designers enjoy high pay and prestige. Those at the top of their profession rarely leave their positions. Therefore, opportunities for newcomers are limited. There always will be more people hoping to break into the field than there are available jobs. Experience working with computer-aided design programs is increasingly important to employers and can help to distinguish a qualified job candidate from the rest of his or her competition. Employment prospects may be better in specialized areas, such as children's clothing. Additionally, openings are more readily available for assistant designers.

FOR MORE INFORMATION

This is a professional membership organization for fashion and accessory designers. Visit the Council's website for industry news and information on scholarships, internships, and its Visiting Designers program, which allows undergraduate students to talk with designers and have their work critiqued.
Council of Fashion Designers of America
http://www.cfda.com

Those interested in creating men's fashions should look at the CTDA's website for business and training information.
Custom Tailors and Designers Association of America (CTDA)
19 Mantua Road
Mt. Royal, NJ 08061

Tel: 856-423-1621
Email: info@ctda.com
http://www.ctda.com

For information about this school, programs, and an application, contact FIT.
Fashion Institute of Technology (FIT)
Seventh Avenue at 27th Street
New York, NY 10001-5992
Tel: 212-217-7999
Email: fitinfo@fitnyc.edu
http://www.fitnyc.edu

This is a professional membership organization for clothing designers and executives. Visit its website to read news about the association and developments in the industry.
International Association of Clothing Designers and Executives
124 West 93rd Street, Suite 3E
New York, NY 10025
Tel: 212-222-2082
Email: newyorkiacde@nyc.rr.com
http://www.iacde.com

Visit the NASD website for a list of accredited art and design schools. Additionally, visit the FAQ: Students, Parents, Public section for useful information on preparing to study art or design in college, applying for financial aid, and accreditation.
National Association of Schools of Art and Design (NASD)
11250 Roger Bacon Drive, Suite 21
Reston, VA 20190-5248
Tel: 703-437-0700
Email: info@arts-accredit.org
http://nasad.arts-accredit.org

For career information, visit the following website:
Career Threads
http://careerthreads.com

For subscription information, visit this magazine's website.
Women's Wear Daily
http://www.wwd.com

INTERVIEW

Kathryn Swan is a handbag designer in Chicago, Illinois. She describes her design style as "'cheeky sophistication—generally clean lines with girly touches, which transition well for being either day or evening bags." She has been a designer for 15 years and has worked full time as the owner/designer of Felix & Agatha for the past two years. (To view her designs, visit http://www.felixandagatha.com.) Kathryn was kind enough to discuss her career with the editors of Careers in Focus: Fashion.

Q. Why did you decide to become a fashion designer?

A. Fashion design was an early dream of mine. I can remember sketching designs and pretending to be a couture designer as early as age 10, but didn't seriously think I could have that job until after college and spent several years in the business world, realizing that wasn't the right path for me. I spent a couple of additional years ramping up my business whilst still at my full-time job before quitting to focus on fashion design as my primary career.

Q. Once you have a design, what are the steps that you take to bring it from idea to finished product?

A. My design process usually begins with an idea that I might sketch out on paper, but I then 'sketch' more fully with fabric as one of the initial steps—basically drafting the preliminary pattern as I work it out three-dimensionally. I'll usually go through a couple of drafts in this manner, starting with a really basic expendable sort of fabric and then in subsequent drafts using a closer version to the actual fabric to be used in final production. I then move on to drafting a paper pattern with specific measurements calculated in and then run a test version of this. The pattern may go through several revisions depending on the specifics of the design. The final pattern is then created and detailed processes documented so the bag can be reproduced.

Q. Can you describe a day in your work life?

A. I start most days by replying to emails or phone calls. The remainder of my time really varies on a day-to-day basis depending on the specific day and week. Rather than spending a specific amount of time each day on every activity, I tend to have certain periods where I'm focused on one activity over the others. I usually spend more time working on designing when I am finishing a new collection of bags and likewise more time responding to wholesale requests after a show or after there has been some press about my line. Paperwork seems to infiltrate all aspects of business, so this is something I tend to address on an ongoing basis, although I prefer to dedicate a day to doing a good portion of it each week so I can complete it all at once rather than dividing it up for the whole week. For me, being able to dedicate the bulk of my attention to one aspect of the business at a time seems to be a better way of making sure everything gets accomplished.

Q. What are some of the pros and cons of work as a fashion designer?

A. This may vary somewhat depending on whether you are starting your own line or working for an established design brand, but in my experience as a designer and small business owner, the biggest pros are autonomy and the ability to use your creativity on a near daily basis. Seeing your ideas come to life is extremely rewarding. I also love the flexibility in scheduling that my job allows me, even though I probably spend more time working now than I ever have in the past. On the flip side, the cons of starting one's own line include the difficulty of establishing a new brand in a market that is already filled with a lot of designers and choices. Other small business–related difficulties also apply to the world of fashion design, particularly issues like finding reasonably priced health insurance when you aren't part of a large group plan.

Q. What is one of the most interesting things that ever happened to you while working as a fashion designer?

A. The past two years of my life as a whole have been the most interesting challenge and reward—just taking the risk to make my dream of being a fashion designer come true. I hear so many people tell me they wish they could do something like I did, but so few people actually risk quitting the security of regular employment to see if they can make it happen. I love that I am every day proving to myself that I can make it work. I learn something new or handle a different challenge nearly every day, and that makes my life and job constantly interesting. Specific highlights include seeing my designs on the runway and having people love designs I've created enough to purchase them for their own collections.

══ INTERVIEW ══

Margaret Voelker-Ferrier is the coordinator of the fashion design program and a professor of fashion design at the University of Cincinnati. (To learn more about the program, visit http://www.daap. uc.edu/program_pdf/sod/BS_FashionDesign.pdf.) She was kind enough to discuss her long and interesting career with the editors of Careers in Focus: Fashion.

Q. Can you tell us about your background in the fashion industry and world of education?

A. At the age of 13, I knew I wanted to be a fashion designer. Was it the Barbie doll, the clothes I made for her and myself, the figure drawings I did all the time from the Barbie booklets, Katie Keene, and *Betty and Veronica* comic books? Or maybe it was the fabulous black and white films of the '40s? Anyway, when I announced to my mother that I was going to be a fashion designer and live in Paris, she said she didn't know where I got my "big ideas." Nevertheless, I held onto those dreams, and when it came time to select a college, I went to the library, looked up fashion design colleges and selected the University of Cincinnati. It had a traditional college campus, offered a bachelor's degree in design, and a very unique opportunity for six cooperative education quarters on the job.

I was accepted into the program and worked in New York, San Francisco, and Cincinnati. After graduation I continued to pursue my goal of living in Paris. I worked a year out of school as a fashion illustrator, and then moved to France. For four years, I worked as a freelance artist and designer. At the end of the fourth year, I realized it was time to make a decision whether I was going to return to the States, or plan to stay forever in Paris. I decided to return to the States, because I had adapted well to France and no matter where I lived, would always live a Francophile lifestyle.

I chose to return to the University of Cincinnati where I was offered a teaching opportunity. All the years I was in Paris, I kept thinking the Fashion Program should incorporate this or that. When I wrote to the chair of the program, she invited me to come teach. I thought this would be a unique experience, and one I had yet to try. First I was a visiting instructor with a one-year appointment. Next, I applied for a tenure-track position and began working on my master's degree in arts administration. In 1986, I received tenure.

From the very beginning of my teaching career, I have loved it. I have always said, I couldn't make up my mind whether I loved drawing or design better . . . here I can do both. The other aspect that is so attractive is the intellectual appeal of deep thinking. Creating new knowledge and working on projects that improve the human condition has been pure joy.

In 1992, I began to put into practice my master's experience of leading the program with a vision for the future. We have added a new track in product development and continue the traditional design track. We have increased enrollment due to demand and the excellence of our program.

Q. Can you provide an overview of the fashion design program at your school?

A. The fashion design program encompasses the two tracks I mentioned above. It is a five-year program with six quarters of practical work experience. The students begin their studies with a foundation of design year that is highly rigorous and covers the basics of design, drawing, and digital drawing software. In addition, they are required to take English, history, art history, psychology, and math. The second year is geared to skills in fashion design—pattern making, fashion drawing, construction, fashion history, textiles, and the fashion industry.

At the end of the second year the student begins the rotation called Co-Op. He/she is sent to a paid position where he/she works for 10 weeks in the industry. This position could be in New York City, Los Angeles, Dallas, Chicago, or Minneapolis. Our students are all over the country, even in Europe. During the next three years, the student will rotate every 10 weeks with a job or school. It is year round: two quarters of work, two quarters of study. In the spring quarter of the fifth year the two sections rejoin and complete their thesis collection project for the final exhibit, fashion show, and graduation.

Q. For what type of jobs does your program prepare students?

A. Because our students move to the city where they work for three months and where they work on "product," the state of Ohio requires they be paid. The companies that pay are typically larger corporations such as Gap, Abercrombie & Fitch, American Eagle, Liz Claiborne, Ellen Tracy, Coach, and Ralph Lauren. Our students are very computer savvy and have exhibited strength in these skills. They can sketch, drape, and make flat patterns. They can research trends, forecast, and create presentations. Ninety percent of this year's graduating class has been hired.

Q. **What are the most important personal and professional qualities for fashion design majors?**

A. A fashion design major should have a love of the tactile—fabrics, work that requires using the hands—as well as a strong capability and love for the third dimension. The product development student should have a strong intuition for trends, researching markets, and making 2D presentations. A strong integrity, love of people, and the desire to seek what is coming would be important personal characteristics.

Q. **What advice would you offer fashion design majors as they graduate and look for jobs?**

A. Create a portfolio that contains the work you like the most. Do not put in things that you do not want to do in the future. Show your strengths first, because the interviewer may be busy and not have time to get to the back where you have your best designs. A portfolio should have a strong beginning that will grab the attention of the viewer, maintain strength with the middle, and a powerful closure so the person will remember you. Do not be pushy, but do speak with confidence in your work. Craft is everything in your presentation. If you care enough to make it, you will care about your job and respect your employer. Take every opportunity to interview with all the people who come to campus. Practice makes perfect. If you have multiple choices, take the one where you will be happiest and can pursue your passion.

Q. **Are there any changes in this job market that students should expect?**

A. Fashion design is a popular field at this time. There are a lot of opportunities—especially when one considers that companies like Abercrombie & Fitch have over 1,000 people creating the intellectual part of their seasons, where 10 years ago they employed only a handful. As long as the U.S. has ownership of the creative side of the industry, the opportunities will continue to be strong.

Another reason clothing has become desirable is that women in the workforce have become powerful. With disposable income and positions of leadership, it is no longer necessary to emulate males for promotion. A woman can be a woman and is free to wear the garments she loves. This in itself has created a desire for luxury goods all over the world.

Q. What is the future of your program?

A. Since this program has been so successful and our graduates generally are offered several thousand dollars more than other graduates, we would like to create more University of Cincinnati programs around the world. We have begun a Center for Design Research and Innovation, where the design opportunities are blending with other fields. This program will enable graduate design students to work together with engineers, business, and medical students to create new ways of solving design problems.

Fashion Illustrators

OVERVIEW

Illustrators prepare drawings for advertisements, magazines, books, newspapers, packaging, websites, computer programs, and other formats. *Fashion illustrators* specialize in distinctive illustrations of the latest women's and men's fashions.

HISTORY

Illustration featured prominently in the ancient civilizations of Mesopotamia, Egypt, and later Greek and Roman civilizations. Drawings depicting knowledge and conveying ideas have also been found among ancient Assyrian, Babylonian, Egyptian, and Chinese societies. Modern illustration began during the Renaissance of the 15th and 16th centuries, with the work of Leonardo da Vinci, Andreas Vesalius, and Michelangelo Buonarotti.

Over time, tools have been developed to aid illustrators in their work. Illustrators have made use of parallel bars, compasses, French curves, and T-squares, but the development of computer technology has largely replaced these mechanical tools with software such as computer-aided design. Today, fashion illustrators combine their artistic skill with technology to produce illustrations that appear in such diverse places as magazines, websites, catalogs, and books.

THE JOB

Fashion illustrators use a variety of media to create illustrations that are used to advertise new fashions (such as clothing, cosmetics, shoes, accessories, and beauty products), promote models, and popularize certain designers. Their illustrations might appear in newspapers such as *Women's Wear Daily;* magazines such as *Glamour, Redbook,* and *Vogue;* books; and in online and print catalogs.

Fashion illustrators work with fashion designers, editors, and models. They make sketches from designers' notes or they may sketch live models during runway shows or other fashion presentations. They may use pencils, pen and ink, charcoal, paint, air brush, computer technology, or a combination of media.

Fashion illustrators who work as freelancers must handle all of the business aspects that go along with being self-employed. Responsibilities might include billing clients, tracking expenditures, purchasing equipment and supplies, and marketing their businesses to ensure that they have new work when their current projects are completed.

REQUIREMENTS

High School

Creative talent is more important in this field than education. However, there are academic programs in illustration at most colleges and universities. If you are considering going on to a formal program, be sure to take plenty of art classes while in high school. Elective classes in illustration, ceramics, painting, or photography are common courses offered at many high schools. If you plan to start your own business, be sure to take business, accounting, and mathematics classes. And be sure to take computer classes as knowledge of computer drawing software and other technology is becoming increasingly important to fashion illustrators. Finally, take as many courses in anatomy and physiology as possible.

Postsecondary Training

To find a salaried position as a fashion illustrator, you should have at least a high school diploma and preferably an associate's or bachelor's degree in fashion illustration, commercial art, or fine art. Illustration studies will include drawing, painting, layout, color, and design. Whether you are looking for full-time employment or freelance assignments, you will need an organized collection of samples of your best work, which is called a portfolio. Employers are especially interested in work that has been published or printed. One advantage of pursuing postsecondary education is that it gives you an opportunity to build your portfolio—which is a collection of your best work. Fashion illustrators should study also clothing construction, cosmetology, fashion design, and anatomy and physiology.

Books to Read

Barron's. *All About Techniques in Illustration.* Hauppauge, N.Y.: Barron's Educational Series, 2001.

Cox, Mary. 2005 *Artist's & Graphic Designer's Market.* Cincinnati, Ohio: Writers Digest Books, 2004.

Edwards, Betty. *New Drawing on the Right Side of the Brain Workbook: Guided Practice in the Five Basic Skills of Drawing.* New York: Jeremy P. Tarcher, 2002.

Fleishman, Michael. *Starting Your Career as a Freelance Illustrator or Graphic Designer.* New York: Watson-Guptill Publications, 2001.

Hagen, Kathryn. *Illustration For Designers.* 2d ed. Portland, Oreg.: Hagen Publishing, 2000.

National Association of Schools of Art and Design Directory 2004. Reston, Va.: National Association of Schools of Art and Design, 2004.

They should also keep up with the latest fashion and illustration trends by reading fashion magazines.

Other Requirements

Fashion illustrators must be creative, and, of course, demonstrate artistic talent and skill. They also need to be flexible since the scope and deadlines of a project may change at the whim of a designer. Because their art is commercial in nature, illustrators must be willing to accommodate their employers' desires if they are to build a broad clientele and earn a decent living. They must be able to take suggestions and rejections gracefully. And, of course, illustrators must have a love of fashion and enjoy expressing style through images.

EXPLORING

You can explore this field by taking drawing classes both at school and through local organizations such as community centers. Also, consider joining your school art club. This club will give you the opportunity to meet with others who share your interests, and they sometimes sponsor talks or meetings with professionals. Join the staff of the school yearbook, newspaper, or literary magazine. These publications often make use of visual art to accompany their text.

Look for part-time or summer work at an art supply store, or assist a professional artist. This work experience will give you the opportunity to become familiar with many "tools of the trade." Explore your interest in the fashion field by reading fashion magazines that will keep you up-to-date on fashion trends, models, and illustrators' work. Try drawing or sewing your own fashion creations. If you can't find work at an art store, try getting a job at a clothing store. This will give you experience working with people and clothes, and you might even be able to suggest fashion advice to customers.

EMPLOYERS

More than half of all professional visual artists (which includes illustrators) are self-employed. Others work for large retailers, magazines, newspapers, design or advertising firms, and fashion firms (called *houses*).

STARTING OUT

Graduates of illustration programs should develop a portfolio of their work to show to prospective employers or clients. Most schools offer career counseling and job placement assistance to their graduates. Job ads and employment agencies are also potential sources for locating work.

ADVANCEMENT

Salaried fashion illustrators advance by being assigned more challenging and unusual work or take on a supervisory position. Others move on to work for more prestigious companies. Freelance fashion illustrators advance by developing a reputation for creativity and the high quality of their work. This allows them to charge more for their services and be more selective about the assignments they take. Fashion illustrators can also go into teaching, in colleges and universities at the undergraduate and graduate levels.

EARNINGS

According to the U.S. Department of Labor, salaried fine artists, including illustrators, had median yearly incomes of approximately $38,060 in 2004. Salaries ranged from less than $17,390 to $68,860 or more annually. Fine artists who were employed in advertising and related services had mean annual earnings of $44,960 in 2004.

Some illustrators can earn several thousand dollars for a single illustration.

Illustrators generally receive good benefits, including health and life insurance, pension plans, and vacation, sick, and holiday pay. Those who work as freelancers do not receive benefits such as health insurance or paid sick or vacation days. Additionally, freelance work is often uncertain because of the fluctuation in pay rates and steadiness of work.

WORK ENVIRONMENT

Although fashion illustrators typically have well-lighted, organized work spaces with room to accommodate their tools, they are also in a fast-paced, deadline-driven environment. They may be required to attend fashion shows and other industry events. Illustrators may often need to put in long or irregular hours to complete an assignment to a client's satisfaction. Freelance illustrators have the added pressure of continually seeking new clients and uncertain incomes.

OUTLOOK

Employment of visual artists is expected to grow about as fast as the average for all occupations through 2012, according to the *Occupational Outlook Handbook*. The outlook for careers in fashion illustration is dependent on the businesses of magazine publishing and advertising. Growth of advertising and public relations agencies will provide new jobs. The popularity of American fashion in other parts of the world will also create a demand for fashion illustrators to provide the artwork needed to sell to a global market.

FOR MORE INFORMATION

This organization is committed to improving conditions for all creators of graphic art and to raising standards for the entire industry.
Graphic Artists Guild
90 John Street, Suite 403
New York, NY 10038-3202
Tel: 212-791-3400
http://www.gag.org

Contact the NASAD for information on accredited arts programs.
National Association of Schools of Art and Design (NASAD)
11250 Roger Bacon Drive, Suite 21

Reston, VA 20190-5248
Tel: 703-437-0700
Email: info@arts-accredit.org
http://nasad.arts-accredit.org

This national institution promotes and stimulates interest in the art of illustration by offering exhibits, lectures, educational programs, and social interchange.
Society of Illustrators
128 East 63rd Street
New York, NY 10021-7303
Tel: 212-838-2560
Email: info@societyillustrators.org
http://www.societyillustrators.org

For career information, visit the following website:
Career Threads
http://careerthreads.com

Fashion Model Agents

OVERVIEW

Fashion model agents act as liaisons between fashion models and their clients. They match models to jobs according to a particular look the client desires. Agents arrange for promising models to work with professional photographers, stylists, and other fashion consultants in order to enhance the models' appearance and develop their style. Agents promote their models to potential clients.

Agents continually look, or "scout," for new models at conventions and modeling contests. They also work at maintaining existing relationships and developing new ones with clients who may offer modeling jobs. Modeling agencies are found in larger cities throughout the United States and abroad, though the larger agencies maintain multiple offices internationally. There are about 92,000 workers employed in the promotion and modeling aspect of the fashion industry; of these, 12 percent hold jobs with modeling agencies or other personnel supply services.

HISTORY

Since the early 20th century, models have been used to show off articles of clothing, shoes, and other accessories. Some models became successful due to the team of professionals working behind the scenes on their behalf. The 1960s saw a number of models become popular celebrity figures, noted not only for their modeling work but also for the image and lifestyle they portrayed. Jean Shrimpton, Twiggy, and Varushka, often referred to as the original "supermodels"—highly paid, internationally famous models—were well known in and out of the fashion industry. In the early days of the fashion industry, models were the products of modeling schools, which also monitored their work schedules. However, as the industry grew and individual models became successful, models often needed, and relied on, someone to manage and organize their careers. Thus, modeling agencies developed to fill this niche.

Ford Models Inc., an agency founded in 1946 by Eileen and Jerry Ford, was one of the first modern agencies devoted to promoting the career of the fashion model. The agency made fashion history by negotiating the first big money contract between model Lauren Hutton and Revlon. Today, Ford Models is an industry leader, employing many talented agents and scouts internationally to represent hundreds of the world's top models.

THE JOB

"Growing up, many of my friends wanted to be models, but I always wondered what it would be like on the other side of the business," says Emily Bartolome, an agent at the modeling agency Aria, located in Chicago.

Models need more than ambition and high cheekbones to get ahead in this industry. They also need an agent. Agents are the link joining the talent (the model) with the employer (clients who have jobs for models). Since clients prefer to work through modeling agencies, most models are represented by one or more agencies.

Bartolome works with about 135 models, some of whom are based in Chicago, others in Los Angeles, Dallas, New York, Miami, and even Canada. Most are between the ages of 16 and 30. While most models work in mainstream fashion (meaning they are typically 5'9" tall and wear size 6), Bartolome does have models doing plus size work (meaning they wear size 14 and up).

An agent's job may begin when a client contacts the agency with a possible job assignment. The client, for example, a retail store or an advertising agency, usually will have a specific "look" in mind for the model. The look may include such aspects as the model's hair color, age group, body type, or ethnicity. Once the specifics have been established, the agent refers to his or her "comp board," an area displaying composite cards of models represented by the agency. Composite cards, used much like business cards, are sheets containing photos of the models in a range of poses and have such information as the model's name, measurements, and agency affiliation. Comp boards are often arranged according to such factors as the models' current locations, hair color, or ethnicity. Comp boards make it easier for agents to locate a particular model for a job.

The agent may then send a group of models to the client for an audition, more commonly known as a "go-see." There are two types of auditions—a general go-see, which means the client requests a specific look (for example, blondes), and a request go-see, which means the client asks for particular models. If the model is chosen for the job, then he or she is booked, or given the assignment.

Many times an agent is also responsible for arranging a photo shoot for the model as well as transportation if the assignment is out of town. A call sheet is a notice containing all pertinent information regarding the modeling assignment, whether it is a photo shoot, fashion show, or product demonstration. Location and time are listed on the sheet, as well as how the model is expected to look—full makeup and styled hair or clean face and hair. Vouchers, detailing the time worked and hourly wage, are signed by the model and client and returned to the agency for billing purposes. The agency is responsible for billing the client and making certain the model is paid for his or her work. In return, the agency earns a commission from the model, which is typically 15 to 20 percent of the model's total earnings, as well as a commission from the client, which is usually about 20 percent. Some larger agencies will advance a weekly or bi-weekly salary until the model's assignments become more regular or the client has paid for the job. Due to the short-lived careers of most models, agents now wisely provide them with financial planning and advice.

Agents spend a considerable amount of time preparing models for work. Newer models often need help with their portfolio, which provides a list of a model's previous assignments and tearsheets (examples of their work "torn out" of magazines or other publications).

Many times, models need professional help in perfecting their image. Bartolome says, "You need to help models develop a look and a sense of style. Many girls are pretty but need some tweaking." Agents may send models to favored stylists for a major change such as a new hairstyle or different hair color. Sometimes, the change may be something subtle such as giving the eyebrows a different arch. Agents may also groom new models in other ways; for example, agents may work to refine the way they walk or carry themselves.

While agents maintain good working relationships with established clients, they also look for new clients and more assignment possibilities. New retail catalogs are just one source for additional job prospects. Says Bartolome, "If we come across a new catalog, we'll call the number, find out where their headquarters are located and where they shoot [the catalog]. Then we send some comp pictures and see if they take a bite."

In addition, agents are continuously searching for new models. Modeling shows and conventions are held through the year all over the United States and abroad. Agents attend such shows to scout for young people, interview and access their modeling potential, and hopefully, sign these promising new talents to modeling contracts.

REQUIREMENTS

High School

A high school diploma is necessary for work as a fashion model agent. If you are interested in pursuing this career, you should concentrate on high school classes such as family and consumer science and art. Take business and mathematics classes since you will be working with contracts and negotiating salaries. English and speech classes will help you develop your communication skills. If your high school offers any sales and marketing courses, be sure to take those. Some high schools offer curriculum targeted to fashion, which may include classes in design, illustration, and sewing. Sign up for these if they're available.

Postsecondary Training

While a college degree is helpful, you don't necessarily need one to get ahead in this industry. Much of the training is learned while on the job. In essence, a model is a commodity you are trying to sell; so naturally, any sales experience you have is good. It's important to believe in and be supportive of your model's potential. "If you're not excited about the talent, it's hard to book the model for work," says Emily Bartolome. Bartolome herself attended Iowa State University and graduated with a bachelor's degree in fashion merchandising. The classes that prepared her for this career included textiles, merchandising and buying, and psychology. On-the-job training may mean working as an assistant, learning to do bookings, keeping track of schedules, and meeting with clients. In this business, your contacts are extremely important. "The fashion world," Bartolome says, "is very much who you know."

Other Requirements

"We work with hundreds of women with different types of egos. It's important to be able to get along with everyone," notes Bartolome. The fashion world is a highly competitive environment filled with individuals who are, more often than not, used to getting their way. The bottom line: If attitude and aggressive behavior easily intimidate you, then this job won't be a good fit.

Agents should be interested in fashion, since they need to stay current on the newest trends of the industry. To do this, agents frequently do a lot of reading during their free time, looking over such magazines as *Vogue* and *Seventeen,* or the trade newspaper *Women's Wear Daily.*

EXPLORING

There are a number of ways you can explore this field while you are still in high school. For example, you can hone your selling abilities by getting a part-time or seasonal job at any retail store. Whether you are selling an article of clothing or a model's talent, what's important is your ability to market and sell a product.

Attend a model convention or search. Elite Modeling Agency, for example, conducts an annual "Look of the Year" contest held in several cities nationwide. You will be able to observe the process potential models go through as well as see agents at work.

Make an appointment with a local modeling agency to shadow an agent for the day. By following an agent wherever he or she goes—bookings, photographers, interviews—you'll get a firsthand view of the professional's busy schedule.

Get actual work experience in the field by applying for any entry-level job at a modeling agency on a part-time or seasonal basis. Even if this means working as the afternoon receptionist, you will have the opportunity to be in the midst of the "action," and more importantly, make contacts for future jobs.

Finally, check out the local library or bookstores for titles covering the fashion industry. Read fashion magazines to familiarize yourself with current looks and big names in the field. Also, check out the Internet for news and articles on fashion.

EMPLOYERS

Modeling agencies employ agents and scouts as well as stylists and photographers. Agencies are located throughout the United States and internationally, though there are established major and minor markets for work. In the United States, the top market is located in New York City, undeniably the fashion capital of the country. Flagship offices of major modeling agencies are located there, such as Ford, Elite, IMG, and Wilhelmina, not to mention top-notch photographers, designers, and advertising agencies. While New York City may offer the best job market and most lucrative bookings, competition for work is intense. Still, many models flock to the city in hopes of making it big. And numerous agents also make their way to the city, hoping to represent those promising new talents.

Miami, Los Angeles, Chicago, Dallas, and Atlanta are also good modeling markets. Chicago offers plenty of commercial work for models. Miami, specifically Miami Beach, is a favorite modeling market due to its great location and weather. The largest modeling markets abroad are Paris and Milan. Again, however, agents face stiff competition for jobs.

STARTING OUT

Don't be afraid to be aggressive in this business. When Emily Bartolome heard that an established modeling agency had come under new ownership, she quickly faxed her resume to their offices. Though she wasn't offered a full-time position right away, she was given the chance to prove her abilities by working as a temp. Two weeks and a successful freelance project later, Bartolome was hired as an agent.

If permanent, full-time positions are unavailable at a particular agency, you might opt to work as an assistant or in a clerical job while you wait for an opening. Another option is to find out from the agency's human resource department what temporary employment agency they use, get a job there, and request to only be assigned to that specific modeling agency. From there, getting noticed is up to you.

One advantage of going to college is that you will be able to use the school's career services office and network with alumni when you are looking for your first job.

ADVANCEMENT

Advancement in this industry can mean representing a larger roster of models or working with more lucrative client accounts. The higher a top model's hourly booking charges, the more the agent's total fee will be. Some agents may choose to move into other areas of the fashion industry and work as a stylist, fashion coordinator, or forecaster of new trends.

Working as a modeling agent is the perfect training ground for sales and management. Experienced and successful agents may opt to open their own agencies representing models, actors, or other forms of talent. Other agents may move outside of the industry and open businesses unrelated to the fashion world.

EARNINGS

Salaries for fashion model agents vary depending on such factors as the agent's experience, the size and location of the agency, and the models represented. New agents can expect to earn an annual starting salary of approximately $26,000. Those with previous agency experience can earn about $45,000 per year or more. Agents at the top of the industry may make in the hundreds of thousands of dollars. Some agencies choose to pay their agents a commission based on fees generated by model/client bookings. These commissions normally range from 10 to 15 percent of booking totals. Weekly salaries based on commissions may vary according to the amount of booking fees generated and collected.

Agents who work on salary generally receive benefits such as paid vacation and sick time, health insurance, and expense accounts to cover work-related travel costs.

WORK ENVIRONMENT

The environment at a modeling agency is fast-paced and exciting. Most days vary in routine, which can be stressful at times. Agents' workspaces are usually clustered together, where comp boards or folios are easily within reach of an agent. Because of this, privacy is at a minimum.

Most agents work about 40 hours a week, Monday through Friday, in clean, well-lit, indoor offices. Their workspace includes a desk, computer, and telephone. Since a large part of the day is spent on the phone conferring with models and clients, some agents opt to wear headsets.

Some travel is expected. Modeling conventions and shows, where young people hope to attract agency attention, are scheduled year-round throughout the United States. An agency's presence at these events is important because agents need to keep abreast of new looks and faces coming onto the fashion scene. Agents also need to be aware of trendy social spots and events and frequently socialize after work. Many models have been "discovered" at dance clubs, restaurants, or high society parties.

While mixing with the fashion elite may seem glamorous and exciting, there is a downside. A small segment of the industry has a reputation for wild living, abusing alcohol and drugs. The agent who wants a long, successful career needs to be levelheaded and able to steer away from such pitfalls.

OUTLOOK

Employment in this field should grow about as fast as the average through 2012. Since most clients prefer to work with modeling agencies, very few models succeed without the support of an agency. New York City will continue to be the hub of modeling in the United States, and many large agencies will stay headquartered there. Agents may find more jobs by representing actors and actresses. Some agents also represent parts models—those that model specific body parts. The most popular parts models specialize in modeling legs, feet, or hands.

Competition for jobs will most likely be stiff since many view the fashion industry as glamorous and high paying. In truth, many careers in this field are short-lived, the result of trends and looks falling out of favor. Only a few supermodels earn millions of dollars in endorsements and reach celebrity status. Most models, on the other hand, achieve more modest successes. Yet agents consider such models the bread and butter of the industry.

FOR MORE INFORMATION

For information about this school, admissions requirements, and exhibitions of the Museum at FIT, contact
   Fashion Institute of Technology (FIT)
   Seventh Avenue at 27th Street
   New York, NY 10001-5992
   Tel: 212-217-7999
   Email: FITinfo@fitsuny.edu
   http://www.fitnyc.edu

This is an organization of training centers for models and talent. Visit its website for information on modeling careers, competitions, and annual conventions.
   International Modeling and Talent Association
   http://www.imta.com

Fashion Photographers

OVERVIEW

Fashion photographers work in the exciting world of fashion. Their skills are focused specifically on styles of clothing and personal image. They take and develop pictures of people, places, and objects while using a variety of cameras and photographic equipment. The photographs are used to advertise new fashions, promote models, and popularize certain designers in both print and electronic formats.

HISTORY

The art of photography goes back only about 150 years. The discoveries that eventually led to photography began early in the 18th century when a German scientist, Dr. Johann H. Schultze, experimented with the action of light on certain chemicals. He found that when these chemicals were covered by dark paper they did not change color, but when they were exposed to sunlight, they darkened. A French painter named Louis Daguerre became the first photographer in 1839, when he invented the daguerreotype. These early images were developed onto small metal plates and did not allow for reproduction of its prints. With the development of negative-based photographic processes, light-sensitive paper was used to make positive multiple copies of the image.

Although the daguerreotype was the sensation of its day, it was not until that late 1800s when George Eastman invented a simple camera and flexible roll film that photography began to come into widespread use by the general public. With the advent of photography, a new media for the promotion of fashion was developed.

QUICK FACTS

School Subjects
Art
Business

Personal Skills
Artistic
Communication/ideas

Work Environment
Indoors and outdoors
One location with some
   travel

Minimum Education Level
Some postsecondary training

Salary Range
$15,390 to $26,610 to
   $54,100+

Certification or Licensing
Voluntary

Outlook
About as fast as the average

DOT
143

GOE
01.08.01

NOC
5221

O*NET-SOC
27-4021.00

Advances in photographic technology enable fashion photographers to use several different cameras, change lenses, and use special filters all in one photo shoot. Technology also allows them to "touch up" the photographs during the developing process or through digital manipulation, removing any unwanted blemish or object from the picture.

THE JOB

Fashion photographers can work in any of several different areas of the fashion field. They provide artwork to accompany editorial pieces in magazines such as *Glamour, Redbook,* and *Seventeen* and newspapers such as *Women's Wear Daily.* The advertising industry is probably the largest employer of fashion photographers who create the pictures that sell clothing, cosmetics, shoes, accessories, and beauty products. Catalog companies employ photographers to provide images that will sell their merchandise through print or online publications.

Fashion photography is a specialized form of photography that requires working on a team with designers, editors, illustrators, models, hair stylists, photo stylists, and makeup artists. Shooting takes place in a studio or on location, indoors and outdoors. Photographers use cameras, film, filters, lenses, lighting equipment, props, and sets. Their first priority is to satisfy the client's requirements. Some photographers develop a unique artistic style that earns them recognition and higher earnings.

Fashion photographers must be artistically talented (able to visualize designs, use colors, and create style) and be adept at using technologies such as digital cameras and various computer programs designed to manipulate photographs.

Photographers may work as freelancers, handling all the business aspects that go along with being self-employed. Such responsibilities include keeping track of expenses, billing clients promptly and appropriately, and keeping their businesses going by lining up new jobs for when a current project ends.

Because the fashion world is extremely competitive and fast-paced, fashion photographers tend to work long hours under the pressure of deadlines and demanding personalities.

REQUIREMENTS

High School

Creativity is probably the most important skill you must have for this field. There are a number of classes you can take in high school to help you determine the extent of your talent as well as prepare you for this work. Naturally, take as many studio art classes as you can. Photography classes will be especially helpful. Also, take computer classes that teach you about photo manipulation software and digital photography. Business, accounting, or mathematics classes will give you skills you will need to keep track of your accounts and run your own business. Take English or communication classes to develop your communication skills. You will be working with a variety of people, often as a member of a team, and you must be able to convey your ideas clearly as well as to follow directions accurately.

Postsecondary Training

Although this is a field in which you don't need to take a specific postsecondary educational route, there are a number of training options available. There are, for example, academic programs in fashion photography at many colleges, universities, and adult education centers. Some community and junior colleges offer associate degrees in photography or commercial art. Photography studies will include shooting and processing techniques using both black-and-white and color film, digital technology, lighting, and composition. An advantage to pursuing education beyond high school is that it gives you an opportunity to build your portfolio. A portfolio is a collection of an artist's best work that shows prospective clients a variety of skills.

In addition to studying art and photography, it is advantageous to study clothing construction, fabrics, fashion design, and cosmetology.

Certification and Licensing

The Professional Photographers of America offers voluntary certification to photographers working in all specialties. Applicants must successfully complete an examination and submit a portfolio of their work.

Other Requirements

Photographers need excellent manual dexterity, good eyesight and color vision, and artistic ability. They need an eye for composition as well as the ability to work creatively. Because they work with groups of people, they will need to be patient, accommodating, and professional. An eye for detail is essential. And, naturally, they should be interested in fashion and expressing style through images.

EXPLORING

To learn more about this field, take photography courses at school or in your community. There are also a variety of contests for young

Books to Read

Frost, Lee. *The A-Z of Creative Photography: Over 70 Techniques Explained in Full*. New York: Watson-Guptill Publications, 1998.

Grimm, Tom, and Michele Grimm. *Basic Book of Photography*. 5th ed. New York: Plume Books, 2003.

London, Barbara, John Upton, Kenneth Kobre, and Betsy Brill. *Photography*. 8th ed. Upper Saddle River, N.J.: Prentice Hall, 2001.

Sammon, Rick. *Rick Sammon's Complete Guide to Digital Photography: 107 Lessons on Taking, Making, Editing, Storing, Printing, and Sharing Better Digital Images*. New York: W. W. Norton & Company, 2003.

Schaub, George. *Using Your Camera, A Basic Guide to 35mm Photography*. Revised ed. New York: Amphoto Books, 2002.

Tarantino, Chris, and Kevin Tan. *Digital Fashion Photography*. Boston: Course Technology, 2005.

people interested in photography. Search the Internet for contests using keywords such as "photography" and "contest." Ask your art teacher or guidance counselor to arrange an information interview with a fashion photographer; perhaps you could even take a tour of his or her studio. You can also learn more about fashion photography by reading fashion magazines and other publications. Study fashion photographs to determine what you like and dislike about each. Finally, look for part-time or summer work at a camera store. This will allow you to work with photographers and become familiar with the "tools of the trade."

EMPLOYERS

More than 50 percent of all professional photographers are self-employed. Others work for large retailers and other companies, magazines, newspapers, design or advertising firms, and fashion firms (called *houses*).

STARTING OUT

If you have received a degree, one of the best ways to start out in this business is to find a job through your school's career services office or by networking with alumni. Those who are interested in photography sometimes gain entry by working as assistants or trainees to established photographers. You may be asked to do such things as move lights, work in the darkroom, and schedule appointments, but you will also gain experience and make contacts in the field. Those who are financially able to do so may go into business for themselves right away. However, it may take considerable time to establish yourself in the field and develop a profitable business.

ADVANCEMENT

Advancement for fashion photographers generally comes as they gain professional recognition. Freelance photographers who become known for the creativity and high quality of their work will have a growing client base. More clients translate into more jobs; more jobs translate into higher earnings. In addition, as photographers become better known, they can charge more for their services and be more selective about what jobs they take. Salaried photographers may either move up within their organization, taking on supervisory roles or working with specific accounts for example, or they may choose to start their own photography business.

EARNINGS

According to the U.S. Department of Labor, the median annual earnings for salaried photographers was approximately $26,610 in 2004. The lowest paid 10 percent made less than $15,390, while the highest paid 10 percent made more than $54,100 per year. Photographers who were employed for newspaper, book, and directory publishers had mean annual earnings of $36,840 in 2004.

Photographers running their own businesses and working on a freelance basis are typically paid by the job. The pay for these jobs may be based on such factors as the photographer's reputation, the prestige of the client (for example, a fashion magazine with an international readership will pay more than a local newspaper doing a Sunday fashion spread), and the difficulty of the work. For some of this work, photographers may make $250 per job. They may also get credit lines and receive travel expenses. As they gain experience, build a strong portfolio of published work, and have prestigious clients, photographers can make $2,000 per job or more. Freelance photographers who have national or international reputations may make in the hundreds of thousands of dollars or more per year. Freelance workers, unlike salaried artists, however, do not have benefits such as health insurance and paid vacation or sick days.

WORK ENVIRONMENT

Photographers' working conditions vary based on the job and the employer. They may need to put in long or irregular hours to meet print deadlines. For some jobs they will work in a comfortable studio, while for others they may be on location, working on a dark street, or in the snow, or at a crowded fashion show. Freelance photographers have the added pressure of continually seeking new clients and uncertain incomes. Establishing oneself in the field can take years, and this is also a stressful process. On the positive side, fashion photographers are able to enjoy working in creative environments where visual images are highly valued.

OUTLOOK

According to the U.S. Department of Labor, employment for visual artists and photographers is expected to grow as fast as the average through 2012. For photographers specifically working in fashion, employment will likely be dependent on the prosperity of agencies involved with the fashion field, such as magazines, newspapers, advertising firms, and fashion houses. The outlook for these agencies currently looks strong. The popularity of American fashions around the world should create a demand for photographers who can effectively capture the latest styles. In addition, numerous outlets for fashion, such as e-zines and retail websites, will create a need for photographers.

Competition for jobs, however, will be keen since these positions are highly attractive to people with artistic ability. In addition, the *Occupational Outlook Handbook* notes that the growing popularity of digital cameras and computer art programs can allow consumers and businesses to produce and access photographic images on their own. Despite this improved technology, the specialized skills of the trained photographer should still find demand in the fashion world. Individuals who are creative and persistent in finding job leads and who are able to adapt to rapidly changing technologies will be the most successful.

FOR MORE INFORMATION

Contact this organization for information on certification, training, competitions, and Professional Photographer *magazine.*

Professional Photographers of America
229 Peachtree Street, NE, Suite 2200
Atlanta, GA 30303
Tel: 800-786-6277
Email: csc@ppa.com
http://www.ppa.com

Contact the society for information on college student membership, careers, and competitions.
Student Photographic Society
229 Peachtree Street, NE, Suite 2200
Atlanta, GA 30303
Tel: 866-886-5325
http://www.studentphoto.com

INTERVIEW

Greg DeBré has been a photographer for 31 years. Approximately 40 percent of his work focuses on fashion. (To view his work, visit http://www.soflaphoto.com.) He discussed his career with the editors of Careers in Focus: Fashion.

Q. Why did you decide to become a photographer?

A. It was the only thing that felt right after my first two years in college taking the "required" courses. I was able to express myself and use my feelings to create something.

Q. What are the most important elements of a successful fashion shoot?

A. Knowing/feeling your lighting. Making the models comfortable. Having GREAT stylists.

Q. Do you travel for your job?

A. Yes. I've worked all over Latin America, the Caribbean, the South Pacific, Southeast Asia, and about 30 states here at home. About 20 percent of my shoots are on location.

Q. What are some of the pros and cons of work as a fashion photographer?

A. Pros: I like shooting the human form . . . I consider it my way of perfecting it. Cons: Many models are primadonnas and are tough to work with. I've thrown a few out of my studio.

Q. What advice would you give to aspiring photographers?

A. As an established photographer said to me when I was in school, "Keep a record of what and how you're shooting." That way you'll know how you created the shots you like and how to not copy the shots you hate. Shoot, shoot, shoot, and then shoot some more!

Fashion Stylists

OVERVIEW

Photo styling is actually an all-encompassing term for the many and varied contributions that a photo stylist brings to the job. Primarily, the photo stylist works with a photographer to create a particular image, using props, backgrounds, accessories, clothing, costumes, linens, and other set elements. Much of the work exists within the print advertising industry, although stylists are also called to do film and commercial shoots. *Fashion stylists* are photo stylists who specialize in helping photographers and other professionals create fashion images. While photo styling may seem like a vague and nebulous profession, it is an increasingly vital part of the photography and advertising industries.

HISTORY

Photo styling has existed since the first photographs were taken. Someone, whether it is a photographer, an assistant, a studio worker, a designer, or an editor, has to make sure all the elements within the frame are arranged in a certain way. Hair and makeup stylists in the film and publishing industries were probably the first to gain recognition (and credit). In fact, most people still associate "styling" exclusively with hair and makeup work, without fully appreciating the contribution of other stylists to the finished photo or film. To this day, photo styling credits are only occasionally listed in fashion and advertising spreads, but that trend is changing. Society is becoming more visually oriented, and the contributions made by stylists are becoming more important. Stylists are gaining the respect of people within the film, television, and print industries. Some photographer/stylist

QUICK FACTS

School Subjects
Art
Business

Personal Skills
Artistic
Communication/ideas

Work Environment
Indoors and outdoors
Primarily multiple locations

Minimum Education Level
Some postsecondary training

Salary Range
$40 to $350 to $500+ per day

Certification or Licensing
None available

Outlook
About as fast as the average

DOT
N/A

GOE
N/A

NOC
5243

O*NET-SOC
N/A

teams are as well-known for their collaborative work as are actors and directors. After toiling in relative obscurity for many years, photo stylists are emerging as powerful voices in industry and in society.

THE JOB

The fashion stylist is a creative collaborator, working with photographers, art directors, models, design houses, and clients to produce a visual image, usually for commercial purposes. It is both a technical and artistic occupation. The kind of work a fashion stylist performs depends upon, among other things, the nature of the photography; the needs of the photographer, studio, and art director; and the requests of the client. Because these factors vary from one situation to another, it is impossible to list all the aspects of a fashion stylist's job. In simple terms, what a stylist does is help to create a "look." The specifics of how it is done are far more complicated.

Prop gathering and set decoration are the most common assignments in photo styling, but stylists have many other responsibilities, each requiring different skills and experience. For example, fashion, wardrobe, and portrait shoots often require a number of professional stylists on hand to scout locations, prepare the set, acquire clothes and accessories, dress the models, and style hair and makeup. *On-figure stylists* fit clothes to a model, and *off-figure stylists* arrange clothes in attractive stacks or against an interesting background. *Soft-goods stylists* introduce appropriate fabric, linens, and clothing into a shoot. *Hair and makeup stylists* are almost invariably cosmetic specialists, and are usually present on any set that employs live models. *Casting stylists* locate modeling talent.

Stylists may also bring special talents to the set, like floral design, gift wrapping, model building, or antiquing. They usually have a "bag of tricks" that will solve problems or create certain effects; a stylist's work kit might include everything from duct tape and cotton wadding to C-clamps and salt shakers. Sometimes a photo stylist is called on to design and build props, perform on-set, last-minute tailoring, even coordinate the entire production from the location search to crew accommodations. The most successful stylists will adapt to the needs of the job, and if they can't produce something themselves, they will know in an instant how and where to find someone who can. Versatility and flexibility are key attributes no matter what the stylist's specialty.

Being prepared for every possible situation is a large part of the fashion stylist's job. Knowledge of photographic techniques, especially lighting, lenses, and filters, can help a stylist communicate better with the photographer. An understanding of the advertising and fashion industries and familiarity with specific product lines and designers are also good tools for working with clients.

Organization is another vital aspect of the fashion stylist's job. Before the shoot, the stylist must be sure that everything needed has been found and will arrive on time at the studio or location. During the shoot, even while working on a model or set, the stylist must be sure that all borrowed materials are being treated with care and that preparations for the next shot are underway. Afterwards, he or she must return items and maintain receipts and records, so as to keep the project within budget. The freelance stylist does all this while also rounding up new assignments and maintaining a current portfolio.

Only part of the stylist's time is spent in photo studios or on location. Much of the work is done on the phone and on the street, preparing for the job by gathering props and materials, procuring clothes, contacting models, or renting other items. For the freelancer, lining up future employment can be a job in itself. A senior stylist working in-house at a magazine may have additional editorial duties, including working with art directors to introduce concepts and compose advertising narratives.

Even during downtime, the stylist must keep an eye out for ways to enhance his or her marketability. The chance discovery of a new boutique or specialty shop on the way to the grocery store can provide the stylist with a valuable new resource for later assignments. Maintaining a personal directory of resources is as essential as keeping a portfolio. Staying abreast of current trends and tastes through the media is also important, especially in the areas of fashion and lifestyle.

What a stylist does on the job depends largely upon his or her unique talents and abilities. Fashion stylists with the most experience and creative resources will make the greatest contribution to a project. As a premier stylist, that contribution extends beyond the set to the society as a whole: shaping its tastes, making its images, and creating art that defines the era.

REQUIREMENTS

High School

There are a number of classes you can take to help prepare you for this career while you are still in high school. Take classes in the visual arts to learn about design and composition. Develop your hand-eye coordination in sculpture or pottery classes where you will be producing three-dimensional objects. Painting classes will teach you about colors, and photography classes will give you a familiarity using this medium. Skill with fabric is a must, so take family and consumer science classes that concentrate on fabric work. You will be able to cultivate your skills pressing and steaming clothes, doing minor alterations, and completing needlework. Because your work as a fashion stylist may require you to work as a freelancer (running your own business) take mathematics classes or business and accounting classes that will prepare you to keep your own financial records. Of course, English classes are important. English classes will give you the communication skills that you will need to work well with a variety of people, to promote your own work, and to drum up new business. The specialties employed for certain shoots require a familiarity with, for instance, formal attire, food preparation, home decorating, children, bedding, and any number of other potential subjects. A fashion stylist, like any artist, draws from his or her own experience for inspiration, so exposure to a wide variety of experiences will benefit anyone entering the field.

Postsecondary Training
There is no specific postsecondary educational or training route you must take to enter this field. Some fashion schools, such as the Fashion Institute of Technology, offer training in fabric styling. Other fashion stylists have attended art schools, receiving degrees in photography; attended fashion schools, receiving degrees in fashion merchandising or a related field; or have entered the field by going into retail, working for large department stores, for example, to gain experience with advertising, marketing, and even product display. The Association of Stylists and Coordinators (ASC) recommends entering the field by working as an assistant for an established stylist. Susan agrees with this recommendation. "Studying photography in college has been helpful," she says, "but I assisted a stylist and got 'on the job' training, which is the best training for a career as a stylist." According to the ASC, such an informal apprenticeship usually lasts about two years. By then, the assistant typically has enough skills and connections to begin working on his or her own.

Other Requirements
The personal qualities most sought in a fashion stylist are creativity, taste, resourcefulness, and good instincts. Stylists work with a variety of people, such as clients, photographers, models, and prop suppliers, and therefore they need to have a calm and supportive

personality. Schedules can be hectic and work is not always done during normal business hours, so stylists need flexibility, the ability to work under pressure, and patience. Stylists who are easy to work with often find that they have a large number of clients. Finally, an eye for detail is a must. Stylists are responsible for making sure that everything appearing in a photo—from a model's hairstyle to the size and color of a lamp—is exactly right.

EXPLORING

There are a number of fun ways to explore your interest in this career. Try teaming up with a friend to conduct your own photo shoot. Arm yourself with a camera, decide on a location (inside or outside), gather some props or costumes, and take a series of photographs. At a professional level, these are known as test shots and are used to build up the portfolios of photographers, models, and stylists. But a backyard photo shoot can be a good way to appreciate the elements involved with this career. Obviously, any opportunity to visit a real photographer's set can be an invaluable learning experience; ask a guidance counselor to help you arrange such a field trip. You should also consider joining a photography or art club. Besides giving you the opportunity to work with the medium, such clubs may also sponsor talks or meetings with professionals in the field.

Look for part-time or summer work in the retail field where you may have the opportunity to set up displays and learn about advertising. Even if you can't find such work, watch someone prepare a display in a department store window. Many stylists start out as window dressers or doing in-store display work.

EMPLOYERS

There are relatively few positions available for full-time, salaried fashion stylists. Some ad agencies, magazines, and companies that sell their merchandise through catalogs have stylists on staff. Most fashion stylists, however, work as freelancers. They are hired for individual assignments by photographers, ad agencies, design firms, catalog houses, and any other enterprise that uses photographic services.

STARTING OUT

A person can enter the field of photo styling at any point in life, but there is no clear-cut way to go about it. Some people, if they have the resources, hire photographers to shoot a portfolio with them, and then shop it around to production houses and other photographers. However, most prospective employers prefer that a stylist has previous on-set experience.

As the ASC recommends, one of the best ways to break into this field is to find work as a stylist's assistant. Production houses and photo studios that employ full-time stylists usually keep a directory of assistants. Most cities have a creative directory of established stylists who may need assistants. It is important to always leave a name and number; they may have no work available immediately, but might be desperate for help next month. Working as an assistant will provide you with important on-set experience as well as show you the nuts and bolts of the job—including the drudgery along with the rewards. Building a reputation is the most important thing to do at any stage of this career, since most photographers find stylists by word of mouth and recommendations, in addition to reviewing portfolios. Assistants will also be introduced to the people who may hire them down the road as full-fledged stylists, giving them an opportunity to make a good impression. Eventually, you can seek out a photographer who needs a stylist and work together on test shots. Once you have enough examples of your work for a portfolio, you can show it to agents, editors, and photographers.

Agency representation can be of enormous help to the freelancer. An agent finds work for the stylist and pays him or her on a regular basis (after extracting an average commission of 20 percent). The benefits of representation is that while a stylist is working one job, the agent is lining up the next. Some agencies represent stylists exclusively; others also handle models, photographers, and actors.

ADVANCEMENT

Advancement in this field can be measured by the amount of bookings a stylist obtains, the steadiness of work, and a regularly increasing pay rate. It can also be determined by the quality of a stylist's clients, the reputation of the photographer, and the nature of the assignments. Some stylists start out with lower-end catalogs and work their way up. If the goal is to work in high fashion, then the steps along the way will be readily apparent in the quality of the merchandise and the size of the client. The opportunity to work with highly regarded photographers is also a step up, even if the stylist's pay rate remains the same. In a career built on reputation, experience with the industry's major players is priceless. Senior stylists at magazines often help in ad design and planning. Some stylists advance to become art directors and fashion editors. Ultimately, each stylist has his or her own goals in sight. The "rare-air" of high fashion and celebrity photography may not be the end-all for all stylists; a good steady income and the chance to work regularly with friendly, creative people may, in fact, be of more importance to a stylist.

EARNINGS

Like almost everything else in this field, earning potential varies from one stylist to the next. Salaries at production houses can start as low as $8 an hour, but usually include fringe benefits like health insurance, not to mention a regular paycheck. The freelancer, on the other hand, has enormous earning potential. An experienced fashion stylist can demand as much as $800 or more a day, depending on his or her reputation and the budget of the production. Regular bookings at this level, along with travel and accommodation costs (almost always paid for), translate into a substantial income.

Most stylists, however, earn less and average approximately $350 to $500 per day. According to the ASC, assistant stylists, who are hired by the day, can expect to make approximately $150 to $200 per day. Neither assistants nor stylists who are freelancers receive any kind of benefits. They must provide for their own health insurance and retirement, and they receive no pay for sick days or vacation days. In addition, while a stylist may have a job that pays $500 a day for several days, there is no assurance that a stylist will find steady employment. It is wise to establish an emergency fund in the event that work disappears for a time. Busy periods often correspond to seasonal advertising campaigns and film work. A stylist might have a great year followed by a disappointing one. Freelancers must file their own quarterly tax returns and purchase their own health insurance.

WORK ENVIRONMENT

Work conditions for a fashion stylist are as varied as the job itself. Preparation for a shoot may involve hours on the telephone, calling from the home or office, and more hours shopping for props and materials to use on the set. Much of the work is done inside comfortable photo studios or at other indoor locations, but sometimes, especially in fashion and catalog photography, outdoor locations are also used. If the merchandise is of a seasonal nature, this could mean long days working in a cold field photographing winter parkas against a snowy background, or it could mean flying down to Key West in January for a week shooting next summer's line of swimwear. Travel, both local and long distance, is part of the job. Days can be long, from dawn to dusk, or they may require the stylist's presence for only a few hours on the set. Hours vary, but a stylist must always be flexible, especially the freelancer who may be called in on a day's notice.

Stress levels vary from one assignment to the next. Some shoots may go smoothly, others may have a crisis occur every minute. Stylists must be able to remain calm and resilient in the face of enormous pressure. Personality clashes may also occur despite every effort to avoid them, adding to the stress of the job. For the freelancer, the pressure to find new work and maintain proper business records are still further sources of stress. Fashion stylists will also spend considerable time on their feet, stooping and kneeling in uncomfortable positions or trying to get something aligned just right. They also may need to transport heavy material and merchandise to and from the studio or location or move these elements around the set during the shoot. Reliable transportation is essential.

The irregular hours of a fashion stylist can be an attraction for people who enjoy variety in their lives. Work conditions are not always that strenuous. The work can also be pleasant and fun, as the crew trades jokes and experiences, solves problems together, and shares the excitement of a sudden inspiration. The rewards of working with a team of professionals on an interesting, creative project is a condition of the job that most stylists treasure.

OUTLOOK

The value of a good fashion stylist is becoming more and more apparent to photographers and advertising clients. However, the outlook for employment for stylists depends a great deal on their perseverance and reputation. Larger cities are the most fertile places to find work, but there are photo studios in nearly every community. The fortunes of the stylist are intrinsically related to the health of the fashion, advertising, film, video, and commercial photography industries—all of which are in good shape. Stylists should try, however, to maintain a wide client base if possible, so they can be assured of regular work in case one source dries up.

Technological advances, especially in the areas of digital photography and photo enhancement, may transform, but not eliminate, the role of the photo stylist in the future. Someday there may be educational avenues for the stylist to enter into the field, and this may increase the amount of competition for styling assignments. Ultimately, though, maintaining the quality of work is the best insurance for continued employment.

FOR MORE INFORMATION

For information on the career of photo stylist, contact
Association of Stylists and Coordinators
18 East 18th Street, #5E
New York, NY 10003
Email: info@stylistsasc.com
http://www.stylistsasc.com

Fashion Writers and Editors

QUICK FACTS

School Subjects
English
Family and consumer science
Journalism

Personal Skills
Artistic
Communication/ideas

Work Environment
Primarily indoors
One location with some travel

Minimum Education Level
Bachelor's degree

Salary Range
$20,000 to $38,000 to
$100,000+ (writers)
$26,490 to $44,620 to
$82,070+ (editors)

Certification or Licensing
None available

Outlook
About as fast as the average

DOT
131, 132

GOE
01.02.01, 01.01.02

NOC
5121, 5122

O*NET-SOC
27-3041.00, 27-3043.00

OVERVIEW

Fashion writers express, promote, and interpret fashion ideas and facts in written form. *Fashion editors* perform a wide range of functions, but their primary responsibility is to ensure that text provided by fashion writers is suitable in content, format, and style for the intended audiences. There are approximately 319,000 writers and editors employed in the United States; fashion writers and editors make a very small percentage of this group.

HISTORY

Starting around the 14th century, fashion trends were promoted via word of mouth and the exchange of fashion dolls. The development of the printing press by Johannes Gutenberg in the middle of the 15th century fostered the growth of printing publications, which eventually lead to publications dedicated to fashion. The first fashion magazine is generally thought to be a German publication that began in the late 16th century.

Fashion writers and editors were originally employed by newspaper, magazine, and book publishers. As technologies changed, fashion writers and editors began to discuss fashion on television and radio shows. Today, fashion writers and editors have a presence on the Web, as well.

THE JOB

Fashion writers, also known as *fashion reporters, correspondents,* or *authors,* express their ideas about fashion in words for books, magazines, newspapers, advertisements, radio, television, and the Internet. These writing jobs require a combination of creativity and hard work.

The majority of fashion writers are employed by fashion magazines. These writers report on fashion news, conduct interviews of top designers, or write feature articles on the latest styles for a season. Fashion writers also work for newspapers with fashion sections (often a part of a larger arts-and-entertainment department), websites, or other media outlets.

Good fashion writers gather as much information as possible about their subject and then carefully check the accuracy of their sources. This can involve extensive library research, interviews, and long hours of observation and personal experience. Writers usually keep notes from which they prepare an outline or summary. They use this outline to write a first draft and then rewrite sections of their material, always searching for the best way to express their ideas. Generally, their writing will be reviewed, corrected, and revised many times before a final copy is ready for publication.

Fashion editors work with fashion writers on the staffs on newspapers, magazines, publishing houses, radio or television stations, and corporations of all kinds. Their primary responsibility is to make sure that text provided by fashion writers is suitable in content, format, and style for the intended audiences. For example, a fashion editor working for a newspaper would ensure that articles are timely and can be understood and enjoyed by the newspaper's average reader—not just people in the fashion industry.

Editors must make sure that all text to be printed is well written, factually correct (sometimes this job is done by a *researcher* or *fact checker*), and grammatically correct. Other editors, including managing editors, editors in chief, and editorial directors, have managerial responsibilities and work with heads of other departments, such as marketing, sales, and production.

REQUIREMENTS

High School

Fashion writers and editors must learn to write well, so it is important to take English, journalism, and communications courses in high school. To gain a better perspective on fashion and design, take classes in family and consumer science, including sewing and design, if they are available in your school. Since much of the fashion industry is based overseas, taking classes in a foreign language, such as French, will also be beneficial. Since all editors and writers use computers, take computer courses and learn how to type quickly and accurately.

Postsecondary Training

A college education is usually necessary if you want to become a writer or editor. You should also know how to use a computer for word processing and be able to handle the pressure of deadlines. Employers prefer to hire people who have a communications, English, or journalism degree. Fashion writers and editors must be knowledgeable about their subject, so classes—or even degrees—in fashion design and marketing are also strongly recommended.

Other Requirements

Good fashion editors and writers are analytical people who know how to think clearly and communicate what they are thinking. They must have the ability to conceptualize in two and three dimensions and convey this information to their audience. They should have a working knowledge of clothing construction and an eye for fashion trends. Fashion editors and writers must keep abreast of the latest styles and movements in the fashion industry.

EXPLORING

To improve your writing skills, read as much as you can. Read all kinds of writing—not just fashion articles. Fiction, nonfiction, poetry, and essays will introduce you to many different forms of writing. Try to write every day. Write your own reviews or articles about the latest fashions or trends in the industry. You can also work as a reporter, writer, or editor on school newspapers, yearbooks, and literary magazines.

EMPLOYERS

Approximately 319,000 writers and editors are employed in the United States. Fashion writers and editors make up only a small percentage of this group. Fashion writers and editors are typically employed by newspaper, magazine, and book publishers; radio and television stations; and online publications. Some fashion writers and editors are also employed by fashion houses and advertising agencies. In the United States, New York City, Miami, and Los Angeles are major fashion centers. Work also may be found in other U.S. cities, although not as many jobs are available in these locations. Many fashion positions are available in foreign countries.

Fashion Publications

CosmoGIRL!
http://www.cosmogirl.com

Cosmopolitan
http://www.cosmopolitan.com

Daily News Record
http://www.dnrnews.com

Elle
http://www.elle.com

Ellegirl
http://www.ellegirl.com

GQ
http://men.style.com/gq

Glamour
http://www.glamour.com

Harper's Bazaar
http://www.harpersbazaar.com

InStyle
http://www.instyle.com

The New York Times: Fashion
http://www.nytimes.com/pages/
fashion

Vogue
http://www.style.com/vogue

W
http://www.style.com/w

Women's Wear Daily
http://www.wwd.com

STARTING OUT

Many fashion writers and editors start out in the industry by gaining experience as *editorial assistants*. Typically, an editorial assistant who performs well will be given the opportunity to take on more and more editorial or writing duties as time passes.

The competition for editorial jobs is great, especially in the fashion industry, so it is important for a beginner who wishes to break into the business to be as well prepared as possible. College students who have gained experience as interns, have worked for fashion publications during the summers, or have attended special programs in publishing will be at an advantage.

Jobs may be found through your school's career services office, classified ads in newspapers and trade journals, specialized publications such as *Publishers Weekly* (http://publishersweekly.com), and Internet sites. Many publishers have websites that list job openings, and large publishers often have telephone job lines that serve the same purpose.

ADVANCEMENT

Employees who start as editorial assistants and show promise may be given a wider range of duties while retaining the same title. Eventually they may become editors or staff writers. They may progress from less significant stories and tasks to important fashion news and feature stories. As they accrue experience, they may be promoted to other editorial or writing positions that come with greater responsibility and pay. They may also choose to pursue managerial positions within the field of fashion editing and writing, such as *managing editor* and *editor-in-chief*. These positions involve more management and decision making than is usually found in the positions described previously. The editor-in-chief works with the publisher to ensure that a suitable editorial policy is being followed, while the managing editor is responsible for all aspects of the editorial department.

As is the case within many editorial and writing positions, a fashion writer or editor may advance by moving from a position on one publication or company to the same position with a larger or more prestigious publication or company. Such moves may involve an increase in both salary and prestige.

EARNINGS

Beginning fashion writers' salaries range from $20,000 to $26,000 per year. More experienced writers may earn between $28,000 and $38,000. Best-selling authors may make $100,000 or more per year, but they are few in number.

The salaries of fashion editors are roughly comparable to those of other editors. Median annual earnings for all editors were $44,620 in 2004, according to the U.S. Department of Labor. The lowest 10 percent earned less than $26,490 and the highest 10 percent earned $82,070 or more. In 2003, the mean annual earnings for editors in newspaper and book publishing were $50,210, while those employed in radio and television broadcasting earned $46,330. Starting salaries of $20,000 or less are still common in many areas.

WORK ENVIRONMENT

The environments in which fashion writers and editors work can vary widely. Most writers and editors work in offices or cubicles. But they may not spend all of their time there, as their job may require them to attend fashion shows in other cities, visit fashion houses or department stores, attend social functions, or make less glamorous visits to the library for research. Many of these events happen after the typical 9 to 5 workday is over, or on weekends.

Almost all fashion writers and editors must deal with deadlines, which affects their work environment. Some writers and editors, such as those who work for newspapers or magazines, work in a much more pressurized atmosphere than those working on books because they face daily or weekly deadlines. Fashion editors and writers working on books may have a more regular 40-hour work-week and less constant deadline pressure, since book production usually takes place over several months. In almost all cases, though, fashion writers and editors will work long hours during certain phases of the editing process to meet deadlines.

OUTLOOK

Employment opportunities in writing and editing are expected to increase about as fast as the average for all occupations through 2012, according to the U.S. Department of Labor. However, because of the narrow scope of fashion writing and editing, competition for jobs will be very intense. Individuals with previous experience and specialized education in fashion and reporting will be the most successful at finding jobs.

FOR MORE INFORMATION

This organization of book publishers offers an extensive website for people interested in learning more about the book business.
Association of American Publishers
71 Fifth Avenue, Second Floor
New York, NY 10003
Tel: 212-255-0200
http://www.publishers.org

For information on the industry, student membership, or networking opportunities, contact
Fashion Group International Inc.
8 West 40th Street, 7th Floor
New York, NY 10018
Tel: 212-302-5511
Email: info@fgi.org
http://www.fgi.org

This organization is a good source of information on internships and the magazine industry.
Magazine Publishers of America
810 Seventh Avenue, 24th Floor
New York, NY 10019

Tel: 212-872-3700
Email: mpa@magazine.org
http://www.magazine.org

For information on educational programs in fashion, contact
National Association of Schools of Art and Design
11250 Roger Bacon Drive, Suite 21
Reston, VA 20190-5248
Tel: 703-437-0700
Email: info@arts-accredit.org
http://nasad.arts-accredit.org

Visit this site for information on careers in fashion writing and editing and school listings
Fashion-Schools.org
http://www.fashion-schools.org

To read about fashions, models, and agencies, check out this website hosted by fashion magazines Vogue *and* W.
Style.com
http://www.style.com

For subscription information, contact
Women's Wear Daily
http://www.wwd.com

Jewelers and Jewelry Repairers

OVERVIEW

Jewelers create, either from their own design or one by a design specialist, rings, necklaces, bracelets, and other jewelry out of gold, silver, or platinum. *Jewelry repairers* alter ring sizes, reset stones, and refashion old jewelry. Restringing beads and stones, resetting clasps and hinges, and mending breaks in ceramic and metal pieces also are aspects of jewelry repair. A few jewelers are also trained as *gemologists*, who examine, grade, and evaluate gems, or *gem cutters*, who cut, shape, and polish gemstones. Many jewelers also repair watches and clocks. There are approximately 40,000 jewelers employed in the United States.

HISTORY

People have always worn adornments of some type. Early cave dwellers fashioned jewelry out of shells or the bones, teeth, or claws of animals. Beads have been found in the graves of prehistoric peoples. During the Iron Age, jewelry was made of ivory, wood, or metal. Precious stones were bought and sold at least 4,000 years ago in ancient Babylon, and there was widespread trade in jewelry by the Phoenicians and others in the Mediterranean and Asia Minor. The ancient Greeks and Romans were particularly fond of gold. Excavations of ancient Egyptian civilization show extremely well crafted jewelry. It was during this time, it is believed, that jewelers first combined gems with precious metals.

Many of the metals jewelers use today, such as gold, silver, copper, brass, and iron, were first discovered or used by ancient jewelers. During the Hashemite Empire, a court jeweler discovered iron while seeking a stronger metal to use in battles. During the Renaissance period in Europe, jewelers became increasingly skillful. Artists such as Botticelli and Cellini used gold and silver with precious stones of every sort to create masterpieces of the gold and silversmiths' trades. Jewelers perfected the art of enameling during this time.

Many skilled artisans brought their trades to Colonial America. The first jewelers were watchmakers, silversmiths, and coppersmiths. In early America, a versatile craft worker might create a ring or repair the copper handle on a cooking pot. By the 1890s, New York City had emerged as a center of the precious metal jewelry industry. It became a center for the diamond trade as well as for other precious stones. The first jewelry store, as we know it today, opened at the turn of the 19th century.

By the early 20th century, machines were used to create jewelry, and manufacturing plants began mass production of costume jewelry. These more affordable items quickly became popular and made jewelry available to large numbers of people.

New York City continues today as a leading center of the precious metals industry and jewelry manufacturing in the United States. Along with Paris and London, New York is a prime location for many fine jewelry designers.

During the 1980s, a small niche of jewelers began creating their own designs and either making them themselves or having other jewelers fabricate them. Also called *jewelry artists,* they differ from more traditional designers both in the designs they create and the methods and materials they use. They sell their designer lines of jewelry in small boutiques, galleries, or at crafts shows or market them to larger retail stores. Many of these jewelers open their own stores. The American Jewelry Design Council was founded in 1990 to help promote designer jewelry as an art form.

THE JOB

Jewelers may design, make, sell, or repair jewelry. Many jewelers combine two or more of these skills. Designers conceive and sketch ideas for jewelry that they may make themselves or have made by another craftsperson. The materials used by the jeweler and the jewelry repairer may be precious, semiprecious, or synthetic. They work with valuable stones such as diamonds and rubies, and precious metals such as gold, silver, and platinum. Some jewelers use synthetic stones in their jewelry to make items more affordable.

The jeweler begins by forming an item in wax or metal with carving tools. The jeweler then places the wax model in a casting ring and pours plaster into the ring to form a mold. The mold is inserted into a furnace to melt the wax and a metal model is cast from the plaster mold. The jeweler pours the precious molten metal into the mold or uses a centrifugal casting machine to cast the article. Cutting, filing, and polishing are final touches the jeweler makes to a piece.

Jewelers do most of their work sitting down. They use small hand and machine tools, such as drills, files, saws, soldering irons, and jewelers' lathes. They often wear an eye loupe, or magnifying glass. They constantly use their hands and eyes and need good finger and hand dexterity.

Most jewelers specialize in creating certain kinds of jewelry or focus on a particular operation, such as making, polishing, or stone-setting models and tools. Specialists include gem cutters; stone setters; fancy-wire drawers; locket, ring, and hand-chain makers; and sample makers.

Silversmiths design, assemble, decorate, or repair silver articles. They may specialize in one or more areas of the jewelry field such as repairing, selling, or appraising. *Jewelry engravers* carve text or graphic decorations on jewelry. *Watchmakers* repair, clean, and adjust mechanisms of watches and clocks.

Gem and diamond workers select, cut, shape, polish, or drill gems and diamonds using measuring instruments, machines, or hand tools. Some work as diamond die polishers, while others are gem cutters.

Other jewelry workers perform such operations as precision casting and modeling of molds, or setting precious and semiprecious stones for jewelry. They may make gold or silver chains and cut designs or lines in jewelry using hand tools or cutting machines. Other jewelers work as pearl restorers or jewelry bench hands.

Assembly line methods are used to produce costume jewelry and some types of precious jewelry, but the models and tools needed for factory production must be made by highly skilled jewelers. Some molds and models for manufacturing are designed and created using computer-aided design/manufacturing systems. Costume jewelry often is made by a die stamping process. In general, the more precious the metals, the less automated the manufacturing process.

Some jewelers and jewelry repairers are self-employed; others work for manufacturing and retail establishments. Workers in a manufacturing plant include skilled, semiskilled, and unskilled positions. Skilled positions include jewelers, ring makers, engravers, toolmakers, electroplaters, and stone cutters and setters. Semiskilled positions include polishers, repairers, toolsetters, and solderers. Unskilled workers are press operators, carders, and linkers.

Although some jewelers operate their own retail stores, an increasing number of jewelry stores are owned or managed by individuals who are not jewelers. In such instances, a jeweler or jewelry repairer may be employed by the owner, or the store may send its repairs to a trade shop operated by a jeweler who specializes in repair work. Jewelers who operate their own stores sell jewelry, watches, and, frequently, merchandise such as silverware, china, and glassware. Many retail jewelry stores are located in or near large cities, with the eastern section of the country providing most of the employment in jewelry manufacturing.

Other jobs in the jewelry business include *appraisers,* who examine jewelry and determine its value and quality; *sales staff,* who set up and care for jewelry displays, take inventory, and help customers; and *buyers,* who purchase jewelry, gems, and watches from wholesalers and resell the items to the public in retail stores.

REQUIREMENTS

High School

A high school education usually is necessary for those desiring to enter the jewelry trade. While you are in high school, take courses in chemistry, physics, mechanical drawing, and art. Computer-aided design classes will be especially beneficial to you if you are planning to design jewelry. Sculpture and metalworking classes will prepare you for design and repair work.

Postsecondary Training

A large number of educational and training programs are available in jewelry and jewelry repair. Trade schools and community colleges offer a variety of programs, including classes in basic jewelry-making skills, techniques, use and care of tools and machines, stone setting, casting, polishing, and gem identification. Programs usually run from six months to one year, although individual classes are shorter and can be taken without enrolling in an entire program.

Some colleges and universities offer programs in jewelry store management, metalwork, and jewelry design. You can also find classes at fashion institutes, art schools, and art museums. In addition, you can take correspondence courses and continuing education classes. For sales and managerial positions in a retail store, college experience is usually helpful. Recommended classes are sales techniques, gemology, advertising, accounting, business administration, and computers.

The work of the jeweler and jewelry repairer may also be learned through an apprenticeship or by informal on-the-job training. The latter often includes instruction in design, quality of precious stones, and chemistry of metals. The apprentice becomes a jeweler upon the successful completion of a two-year apprenticeship and passing written and oral tests covering the trade. The apprenticeship generally focuses on casting, stone setting, and engraving.

Most jobs in manufacturing require on-the-job training, although many employers prefer to hire individuals who have completed a technical education program.

Certification or Licensing

Certification is available in several areas through the Jewelers of America, a trade organization. Those who do bench work (the hands-on work creating and repairing jewelry) can be certified at one of four levels: certified bench jeweler technician, certified bench jeweler, certified senior bench jeweler, and certified master bench jeweler. Each certification involves passing a written test and a bench test. Jewelers of America also offers certification for management and sales workers. Although voluntary, these certifications show that a professional has met certain standards for the field and is committed to this work.

Other Requirements

Jewelers and jewelry repairers need to have extreme patience and skill to handle the expensive materials of the trade. Although the physically disabled may find employment in this field, superior hand-eye coordination is essential. Basic mechanical skills such as filing, sawing, and drilling are vital to the jewelry repairer. Jewelers who work from their own designs need creative and artistic ability. They also should have a strong understanding of metals and their properties. Retail jewelers and those who operate or own trade shops and manufacturing establishments must work well with people and have knowledge of merchandising and business management and practices. Sales staff should be knowledgeable and friendly, and buyers must have good judgment, self-confidence, and leadership abilities. Because of the expensive nature of jewelry, some people working in the retail industry are bonded, which means they must pass the requirements for an insurance company to underwrite them.

EXPLORING

If you are interested in becoming a jeweler or jewelry repairer, you can become involved in arts and crafts activities and take classes in crafts and jewelry making. Many community education programs are available through high schools, park districts, or local art stores and museums. Hobbies such as metalworking and sculpture are useful in becoming familiar with metals and the tools jewelers use. Visits to museums and fine jewelry stores to see collections of jewelry can be helpful.

If you are interested in the retail aspect of this field, you should try to find work in a retail jewelry store on a part-time basis or during the summer. A job in sales, or even as a clerk, can provide a firsthand introduction to the business. A retail job will help you become familiar with a jewelry store's operations, its customers, and the jewelry sold. In addition, you will learn the terminology unique to the jewelry field. Working in a store with an in-house jeweler or jewelry repairer provides many opportunities to observe and speak with a professional engaged in this trade. In a summer or part-time job as a bench worker or assembly line worker in a factory, you may perform only a few of the operations involved in making jewelry, but you will be exposed to many of the skills used within a manufacturing plant.

You also may want to visit retail stores and shops where jewelry is made and repaired or visit a jewelry factory. Some boutiques and galleries are owned and operated by jewelers who enjoy the opportunity to talk to people about their trade. Art fairs and craft shows where jewelers exhibit and sell their products provide a more relaxed environment where jewelers are likely to have time to discuss their work.

EMPLOYERS

Jewelers work in a variety of settings, from production work in multinational corporations to jewelry stores and repair shops. Some jewelers specialize in gem and diamond work, watchmaking, jewelry appraisal, repair, or engraving, where they may work in manufacturing or at the retail level. Other jewelers work only as appraisers. In most cases, appraisals are done by store owners or jewelers who have years of experience. About one-fourth of all jewelers are self-employed. The majority of the self-employed jewelers own their own stores or repair shops or specialize in designing and creating custom jewelry. Top states for jewelry manufacturing include Rhode Island, New York, and California.

STARTING OUT

A summer or part-time job in a jewelry store or the jewelry department of a department store will help you learn about the business. Another way to enter this line of work is to contact jewelry manufacturing establishments in major production centers. A trainee can acquire the many skills needed in the jewelry trade. The number of trainees accepted in this manner, however, is relatively small. Students who have completed a training program improve their chances of finding work as an apprentice or trainee. Students may learn about available jobs and apprenticeships through the career services offices of training schools they attend, from local jewelers, or from the personnel offices of manufacturing plants.

Those desiring to establish their own retail businesses find it helpful to first obtain employment with an established jeweler or a manufacturing plant. Considerable financial investment is required to open a retail jewelry store, and jewelers in such establishments find it to their advantage to be able to do repair work on watches as well as the usual jeweler's work. Less financial investment is needed to open a trade shop. These shops generally tend to be more successful in or near areas with large populations where they can take advantage of the large volume of jewelry business. Both retail jewelry stores and trade shops are required to meet local and state business laws and regulations.

ADVANCEMENT

There are many opportunities for advancement in the jewelry field. Jewelers and jewelry repairers can go into business for themselves once they have mastered the skills of their trade. They may create their own designer lines of jewelry that they market and sell, or they can open a trade shop or retail store. Many self-employed jewelers gain immense satisfaction from the opportunity to specialize in one aspect of jewelry or to experiment with new methods and materials.

Workers in jewelry manufacturing have fewer opportunities for advancement than in other areas of jewelry because of the declining number of workers needed. Plant workers in semiskilled and unskilled positions can advance based on the speed and quality of their work and by perseverance. On-the-job training can provide opportunities for higher-skilled positions. Workers in manufacturing who show proficiency can advance to supervisory and management positions, or they may leave manufacturing and go to work in a retail shop or trade shop.

The most usual avenue of advancement is from employee in a factory, shop, or store to owner or manager of a trade shop or retail store. Sales is an excellent starting place for people who want to own their own store. Sales staff receive firsthand training in customer relations as well as knowledge of the different aspects of jewelry store merchandising. Sales staff may become gem experts who are qualified to manage a store, and *managers* may expand their territory from one store to managing several stores in a district or region. Top management in retail offers many interesting and rewarding positions to people who are knowledgeable, responsible, and ambitious. Buyers may advance by dealing exclusively with fine gems that are more expensive, and some buyers become *diamond merchants,* buying diamonds on the international market.

Jewelry designers' success depends not only on the skill with which they make jewelry but also on the ability to create new designs and keep in touch with current trends in the consumer market. Jewelry designers attend craft shows, trade shows, and jewelry exhibitions to see what others are making and to get ideas for new lines of jewelry.

EARNINGS

Jewelers and precious stone and metal workers had median annual earnings of $27,870 in 2004, according to the U.S. Department of Labor. Salaries ranged from less than $16,670 to more than $48,280. Most jewelers start out with a base salary. With experience, they can charge by the number of pieces completed. Jewelers who work in retail stores may earn a commission for each piece of jewelry sold, in addition to their base salary.

Most employers offer benefit packages that include paid holidays and vacations and health insurance. Retail stores may offer discounts on store purchases.

WORK ENVIRONMENT

Jewelers work in a variety of environments. Some self-employed jewelers design and create jewelry in their homes; others work in small studios or trade shops. Jewelers who create their own designer lines of jewelry may travel to retail stores and other sites to promote their merchandise. Many designers also attend trade shows and exhibitions to learn more about current trends. Some sell their jewelry at both indoor and outdoor art shows and craft fairs. These shows are held on weekends, evenings, or during the week. Many jewelry artists live and work near tourist areas or in art communities.

Workers in jewelry manufacturing plants usually work in clean, air-conditioned, and relatively quiet environments. Workers in departments such as polishing, electroplating, and lacquer spraying may be exposed to fumes from chemicals and solvents. Workers who do bench work sit at workstations. Other workers stand at an assembly line for many hours at a time. Many workers in a manufacturing plant perform only one or two types of operations so the work can become repetitive. Most employees in a manufacturing plant work 35-hour workweeks, with an occasional need for overtime.

Retail store owners, managers, jewelers, and sales staff work a variety of hours and shifts that include weekends, especially during the Christmas season, the busiest time of year. Buyers may work more than 40 hours a week because they must travel to see wholesalers. Work settings vary from small shops and boutiques to large department stores. Most jewelry stores are clean, quiet, pleasant, and attractive. However, most jewelry store employees spend many hours on their feet dealing with customers, and buyers travel a great deal.

OUTLOOK

Employment of jewelers is expected to grow more slowly than the average through 2012, according to the *Occupational Outlook Handbook*. Consumers now are purchasing jewelry from mass marketers, discount stores, catalogs, television shopping shows, and the Internet as well as from traditional retail stores. This may result in store closings or limited hiring. However, jewelers and jewelry repairers will continue to be needed to replace those workers who leave the workforce or move to new positions. Since jewelry sales are increasing at rates that exceed the number of new jewelers entering the profession, employers are finding it difficult to find skilled employees.

The number of workers in manufacturing plants is declining because of increased automation, but opportunities in retail should remain steady or improve slightly. Demand in retail is growing for people who are skilled in personnel, management, sales and promotion, advertising, floor and window display, and buying.

FOR MORE INFORMATION

For industry information, contact
American Jewelry Design Council
760 Market Street, Suite 900
San Francisco, CA 94102
http://www.ajdc.org

For an information packet with tuition prices, application procedures, and course descriptions, contact
Gemological Institute of America
The Robert Mouawad Campus
5345 Armada Drive
Carlsbad, CA 92008
Tel: 800-421-7250
Email: admissions@gia.edu
http://www.gia.edu

For certification information, a school directory, and a copy of
Careers in the Jewelry Industry, *contact*
Jewelers of America
52 Vanderbilt Avenue, 19th Floor
New York, NY 10017
Tel: 646-658-0246
Email: info@jewelers.org
http://www.jewelers.org

For career and school information, contact
Manufacturing Jewelers and Suppliers of America
45 Royal Little Drive
Providence, RI 02904
Tel: 800-444-6572
Email: mjsa@mjsainc.com
http://www.mjsainc.com

Knit Goods Industry Workers

OVERVIEW

Knit goods industry workers set up, operate, and repair the machines that knit various products, such as sweaters, socks, hats, sweatshirts, undergarments, lace, and other garments. The work is distinct from weaving, in that knitting consists of drawing one strand of yarn through the loops of another with needles, while weaving builds fabric by interlocking threads at right angles to each other. There are approximately 1.1 million textile, apparel, and furnishings workers employed in the United States.

HISTORY

Knitting and weaving are two distinct and separate crafts. Weaving is quite ancient, while knitting was not introduced to Europe until sometime in the 1400s. The first knitting machine was invented in England in 1589. Other forms of knitting include lace making and crocheting.

Although many people enjoy knitting special gifts and articles of clothing by hand as a hobby, a large knitting industry powered by automatic machinery has grown to satisfy the need for all types of knitted goods. Historically, because cotton was and is produced primarily in the Southern states, heavy industries such as knitting and textile mills were situated near the cotton; this was cheaper than shipping the cotton to mills in the North. Many regional specialties, however, have arisen over time.

QUICK FACTS

School Subjects
Computer science
Family and consumer science

Personal Skills
Following instructions
Mechanical/manipulative

Work Environment
Primarily indoors
Primarily one location

Minimum Education Level
Apprenticeship

Salary Range
$15,380 to $23,840 to $31,680+

Certification or Licensing
None available

Outlook
Decline

DOT
685

GOE
08.03.01

NOC
9442

O*NET-SOC
51-6031.00, 51-6031.01, 51-6031.02, 51-6051.00, 51-6061.00, 51-6062.00, 51-6063.00, 51-6064.00

THE JOB

Two different methods can be used in the manufacture of knit goods: the cut-and-sew method and the full-fashioned method. While both of these employ some of the same types of machine operators, they also have certain employees that are unique to each.

With the *cut-and-sew method,* the various parts of the knit product, such as sleeves, body, and collar, are made separately, dyed, trimmed, and then sewn together. The first step is to adjust the knitting machine to produce the type and pattern of knit that the product requires. Automatic knitting looms are controlled in a number of ways, usually by metal plates, cards, tapes, or chains that control the operation of the needles. On a Jacquard, or Jacquard loom machine (named after its French inventor), the knit pattern is controlled by holes punched in metal plates. The *Jacquard-plate maker* will snap small covers over particular holes in a pattern plate, then link plates together to form a continuous chain. The Jacquard-plate maker and the *knitter mechanic* then work together to install the plates in the knitting machine and start a trial run to determine that the specified knit pattern is being produced. While the needles are controlled in this manner, the guide bars (flat metal bars on which yarn guides are attached) are controlled by pattern chains assembled by the *pattern assembler.* Patterns can also be dictated by pattern wheels that control the operation of the needles in circular knitting machines. Needle jacks are inserted in notches in the pattern wheel by the *pattern wheel maker,* who sometimes marks the top of the pattern wheel to indicate where the pattern begins.

After the patterns are installed, the knitting-machine operator tends the machine as it turns yarn into the basic parts for garments. Often an operator will tend more than one machine. Spools of yarn are placed on the creel (spindles for holding bobbins) of the machine, and the yarn is threaded through the needles, yarn guides, tension springs, and carriers, using a hook. The operator then ties the new yarn to the ends of the old yarn still in place and activates the machine to knit a small piece of cloth, or a false start, to thread the new yarn into the machine. The operator laps this false start around a take-up roller, adjusts the counters on the machine to produce a certain number of pieces, and activates the machine. While the machine is working, the operator checks to be sure there are no flaws in the knitting and that the yarn threads don't break or run out.

Knitted sections are collected on the take-up roller or are folded and stacked into bundles as they come out of the machine. After a certain number, the operator will take a roll or bundle and attach a tag that specifies the lot number, size, color, and number of pieces. The bundles are then weighed, bundled, or packed into sacks, and sent to the laundry or dye house. The operator then resets the knitting machine and inspects it for routine maintenance before starting a new lot. Routine maintenance can include replacing broken needles, emptying waste oil, refilling oil cups, and greasing machine parts.

In larger plants, regular maintenance of the machines is the job of the *knitting-machine fixer,* who can also set up a machine to produce a certain fabric pattern like the knitter mechanic. The fixer will observe the machine in operation and turn set screws and handwheels to adjust the gears and cams of the machine. The fixer also repairs or replaces broken machine parts; aligns and straightens needles, sinkers, and dividers; and cleans and oils the machine.

After knitting, the garment parts must be cleaned and softened. The *knit-goods washer* runs the knitted tubular cloth through a machine that washes it with detergent and treats it with fabric-softening chemicals. If the cloth is made of undyed yarn, it must be cleaned and specially treated before it is dyed. The cloth is again bundled into sacks, cleaned, and bleached if the garment is to be white or pastel colors. The bags are then taken to be dyed by the *dye-tub operator.* The operator fills the dye machine with water and steam to a specified level; pours in the dye, cleaning agent, or finishing chemicals; sets the temperature and dyeing time according to the formula; places the cloth into the compartments of the machine; and submerges the cloth into the dye. After the specified dyeing time, the tubs are drained and then refilled for a second scouring cycle to remove excess dye from the material. Fabric softeners and finishing chemicals are then added in the final rinse. The dyed fabric is then sent to *drying-machine operators* who tumble dry it in machines and send it to the people who assemble the pieces into whole garments. The cloth may also be brushed to impart a certain nap or feel.

On their way from the dye house, the *garment steamer* removes wrinkles from the fabric pieces with a machine that emits steam and hot air. The knit cloth at this stage is still in long, tubular form. Most often the cloth needs to be slit open, laid flat, cut into the proper pieces, and then sewn together. The *tubular-splitting-machine tender* cuts the fabric to flatten it out, watching carefully for defective splitting. The fabric is then laid out in layers so the *pattern marker* can examine the fabric and mark the material for cutting the garment pieces. Next, *machine cutters* use round knives or band knives to cut the pieces that will be sewn together to make the finished garment.

The pieces are bundled together according to lot and sent to the *overedge sewer*, who puts them through a sewing machine equipped with a rotary cutter to trim the raw cuts and loose threads. At the same time, the machine sews the edges with an overedge stitch for decoration and for the prevention of unraveling. The garment pieces are then taken to the *sewing-machine operator* to be sewn together. Finally, labels, buttons, and any other small items are sewn to the garment, which is then inspected and packed for shipment.

The second method of manufacturing knit goods—the full-fashioned method—produces items that are knitted in one piece, such as fancy sweaters, socks, hats, and scarves. A few special steps are required in this method, which can be described using a sweater as an example. The bottom edge and cuffs of the sweater are first made on flat knitting machines. The *topper* loops the stitches of these ribbed sweater parts onto the points of a transfer bar, which makes it easy to transfer the part to the needles of the knitting machine. The transfer bar will hold several ribbed parts, separated by lengths of loose yarn that is not knitted, so that several sweaters can be knitted in succession. The *full-fashioned garment knitter* takes the transfer bar, positions it over the needle bed of the knitting machine, and pushes the stitches from transfer points onto the machine needles. The transfer bar can then be removed. The knitter operates the knitting machine, which is specially programmed to increase or decrease stitching at specified points in the garment. For example, stitching starts low at the point where the sweater hooks up with its linked bottom, increases in the body of the sweater, and then decreases at the shoulders and sleeves to narrow the sweater. This can happen automatically or by the action of the knitter. The sweater is then taken off the machine and another is started.

The sweater is sent to the *looper*, who operates a looping machine to attach the collar and to shape the sweater further. The needles of the machine can impart a chain stitch along the shoulders, armholes, sleeves, and collar of the sweater, which sharpens the contours and shape of the sweater, making it look more like a cut-and-sewn sweater. The sweater is then cleaned, dyed, softened, and finished in the same manner as described for the cut-and-sew method.

REQUIREMENTS

High School

Most of the production jobs in the knit goods industry are learned on the job, although the basic skills involved can be learned in high school or technical school. Although most employers prefer to hire high school graduates, it is not absolutely required. Technology is increasing in the knitting industry and other textile industries, and this will create a demand for employees with solid educational backgrounds. The machines that perform stitch-making and assembly may be computer controlled. Color patterns for garments can also be computer controlled.

If you are interested in a job in this industry, consider taking computer courses and electronics shop classes in high school to prepare for the technical aspects of this work. Basic mathematics classes or shop mathematics will also give you an educational edge. Develop your blueprint reading and drawing abilities through shop or drafting classes. Since you will be working with knit goods, consider taking any family or consumer science courses that allow you to work with fabrics or yarns, perhaps creating your own articles of clothing to see what is involved in the process. Finally, don't forget to take English classes. These classes will help you hone your researching, reading, and writing skills, which you will need for following repair manuals and when you reach positions of greater responsibility.

Postsecondary Training

Programs in textile design and textile technology are offered at many technical schools and two-year colleges. There, cutters can learn pattern making, cutting, and pattern grading.

Apprenticeships for knitters and other craftspeople in the knitting industry are generally available. Information on apprenticeships can be obtained from the regional offices of the U.S. Department of Labor's Employment and Training Administration (http://www.doleta.gov/atels_bat) and state employment offices, as well as by contacting textile and apparel companies directly. Training periods vary significantly from job to job and from mill to mill. Training may be as short as a few days for a cleaner or as long as several months for a machine tender. For certain occupations, such as sewing machine operators and steamers, piecework pay is used as an incentive so that once the employee has mastered the job, he or she is motivated to work swiftly.

Other Requirements

You will need to have good manual dexterity as well as enjoy working with machinery to do this job well. Because you may often be working on your feet or working in awkward positions to repair machinery, physical stamina is a necessary characteristic. Many factories operate 24 hours a day; because of this schedule, you may be required to work a variety of shifts, sometimes changing between daytime and nighttime work. Finally, because you may be checking the patterns of the knit goods being produced, your position may require you to have good color vision.

EXPLORING

Some state employment agencies operate programs that allow you the chance to take high school courses and participate in on-the-job training in various occupations in the knit goods industry. You should contact your state agencies for information on these types of programs and other part-time or summer jobs available. Unions, such as UNITE HERE, are also a good source of information on jobs in the industry. Since these jobs involve repairing machinery and keeping it in good running condition, consider joining a club or taking a class at a community center that focuses on mechanics. You may be able to work on cars, bikes, or even lawn mowers while learning valuable tips from instructors.

EMPLOYERS

Approximately 1.1 million textile, apparel, and furnishings workers are employed in the United States. While there are knitting mills in every state in the union, nearly 60 percent of all those employed in the textile industry work in North Carolina, South Carolina, and Georgia. Mills in the Northeast produce most of the country's sweaters, while those in the Southeast produce most of our knit sportswear. Most of the country's underwear is produced in the Southeast and in eastern Pennsylvania, while most of our socks and stockings come from North Carolina, which has 80 percent of the nation's hosiery mills.

STARTING OUT

People with production jobs in the knit goods industry start from the bottom as helpers and apprentices and work their way up. Technical school or two-year college graduates may be able to find work through school placement offices. To find out about job openings, job seekers can contact the knitting mills directly or find out more through a state employment agency or union office.

ADVANCEMENT

After an apprenticeship period, workers can move from an apprentice knitter to an assistant knitter to a skilled knitter. Workers can also move from their present job to one that offers more skilled or higher paying work. For example, a floor worker who moves material between the areas of the mill can train for and move into a job as a sewing machine operator.

Workers who have proven themselves with their machinery can advance in several ways. Some become instructors and train new employees. Others advance by taking positions requiring more skills and greater responsibility. Because machine operators and setup crews are the most highly skilled production workers, first-line supervisory positions are usually filled from their ranks. Most companies have training programs to help interested employees advance; many pay all or part of the tuition for work-related courses.

EARNINGS

The earnings of knitting mill workers vary according to the mill they work in and the goods they produce. The U.S. Department of Labor reported the median hourly earnings for textile knitting and weaving machine setters, operators, and tenders to be $11.46 in 2004. This wage translates into yearly earnings of approximately $23,840 based on a 40-hour workweek. Salaries ranged from less than $16,540 to more than $31,480. Textile cutting machine setters, operators, and tenders earned $10.22 an hour (or $21,260 annually). Salaries ranged from less than $15,380 to more than $31,680. Workers in hosiery plants and knit outerwear and knit underwear mills normally earn less. Many production workers in apparel manufacturing are paid according to the number of pieces they produce, so their total earnings depend on skill, speed, and accuracy. Apprentices are normally paid wages somewhat lower than experienced employees.

Benefits, like wages, can vary depending on the mill and the union contract. They usually include paid holidays and vacations, health and life insurance, retirement plans, sick leave, and educational reimbursement. Additionally, most companies operate company stores in which employees can get discounts on the goods the company produces.

WORK ENVIRONMENT

Working conditions depend on the age of the mill and its degree of modernization. Newer buildings have better ventilation and temperature control equipment that reduces some of the problems caused by dust and fumes. Workers in areas with high levels of dust or fumes wear safety glasses and masks that cover their noses and mouths.

Although some of the newer knitting machinery has reduced the level of noise in mills, workers in some areas must still wear earplugs.

The usual workweek in a knitting mill is from 35 to 40 hours. Knitters usually work longer shifts, however, sometimes up to 60 hours a week. Workers may be laid off during slow seasons.

This work can be very repetitious. Physical stamina is required because machine operators are on their feet much of the time. Knitters must have good eyesight to spot dropped stitches and broken threads, and the agility and alertness to tend many machines at once.

Although there are safety features on all new machinery, the knit goods industry worker needs to pay continual attention to the job. With steamers, cutters, and dye tubs, the equipment can inflict harm when used improperly.

Small family-run businesses can be quiet, friendly environments, with most of the knitting done by hand. The work can be difficult, though, and the pay is usually quite low. Today, most handmade garments come from foreign countries.

OUTLOOK

Employment prospects for knit goods workers and other textile workers are not expected to be strong. In fact, the U.S. Department of Labor predicts a decline in employment for knit goods industry workers through 2012. While the demand for knit goods has increased along with population growth, automation and competition from overseas have combined to keep the demand for knit goods workers down. The number of jobs in knitting mills has decreased significantly in the last 10 years as the result of plant closings and downsizing.

The continuing growth of imports can be expected to prompt greater industry specialization. Companies will concentrate on manufacturing products in which they have a competitive advantage. Labor-saving, computerized machinery has increased productivity. Job prospects look best for skilled engineers, technicians, computer personnel, and others who know how to operate and service complex knitting machinery.

FOR MORE INFORMATION

This trade association is for U.S. companies that manufacture and sell synthetic and cellulosic fibers.
American Fiber Manufacturers Association
1530 Wilson Boulevard, Suite 690
Arlington, VA 22209

Tel: 703-875-0432
Email: afma@afma.org
http://www.afma.org

This national trade association for the U.S. textile industry has member companies in more than 30 states that process about 80 percent of all textile fibers consumed by plants in the United States. It works to encourage global competitiveness and increase foreign market access.
National Council of Textile Organizations
910 17th Street, NW, Suite 1020
Tel: 202-822-8028
Washington, DC 20006
http://www.ncto.org

This union fights for workers' rights. It represents workers in various industries, including basic apparel and textiles.
UNITE HERE
275 7th Avenue
New York, NY 10001-6708
Tel: 212-265-7000
http://www.unitehere.org

For career information, visit the following website
Career Threads
http://careerthreads.com

Makeup Artists

QUICK FACTS

School Subjects
Art
Theater/dance

Personal Skills
Artistic
Communication/ideas

Work Environment
Indoors and outdoors
Primarily multiple locations

Minimum Education Level
Some postsecondary training

Salary Range
$13,410 to $24,410 to
$100,000+

Certification or Licensing
None available

Outlook
Faster than the average

DOT
333

GOE
01.06.02

NOC
5226

O*NET-SOC
39-5091.00

OVERVIEW

Makeup artists prepare models and actors for performances on stage and before cameras.

HISTORY

Theatrical makeup is as old as the theater itself. Cultures around the world performed ritualistic dances, designed by spiritual leaders, to communicate with gods and other supernatural forces. These dances often involved elaborate costumes and makeup. By the Elizabethan age, theater had become an entertainment requiring special makeup techniques to transform the male actors into female characters. In Asia in the 17th century, Kabuki theater maintained the symbolic origins of the drama; actors wore very stylized makeup to depict each character's nature and social standing. It wasn't until the late 18th century in Europe that plays, and therefore costumes and makeup, were based on realistic portrayals of society. The grease stick, a special makeup stick that could withstand harsh stage lights without smearing, was invented in the 19th century.

This grease stick led the way for other advancements in the chemistry of stage makeup, but even today's makeup artists must use ingenuity and invention to create special effects. With the advent of filmmaking came new challenges in makeup design—artists were required to create makeup that would not only hold up under intense lighting, but would look realistic close up.

As the fashion industry emerged in the early 20th century, makeup artists were needed to assist models look their best for fashion shoots and shows. Today, fashion makeup artists are key professionals in the fashion industry.

THE JOB

Makeup artists who work in the fashion industry prepare models for photo shoots, fashion shows, and other fashion industry events. They often collaborate with designers to create makeup and hair "looks" for seasonal collections. In addition to applying makeup, in smaller markets, makeup artists are often responsible for styling hair, extensions, and wigs. Outside of the fashion industry, makeup artists are employed in the motion picture, television, and commercial industries, as well as in theatrical productions.

Makeup artists work in a variety of settings. They might work a fashion shoot one day, a runway show the next, and on a commercial set the following day. Some makeup artists may also work for department stores, demonstrating cosmetics to customers.

In addition to artistic responsibilities, freelance makeup artists must handle all of their own administrative tasks such as updating their portfolio and websites, shopping for supplies in stores and online, managing their calendar, running errands, and invoicing clients.

REQUIREMENTS

High School

Does working as a makeup artist sound interesting to you? If so, there are a number of classes you can take in high school to help prepare you for this profession. Take all the art classes you can, including art history if this is offered at your school. Photography courses will help you understand the use of light and shadow. Courses in illustration, painting, and drawing will help you to develop the skills you'll need for illustrating proposed makeup effects. Other helpful classes for you to take are anatomy and chemistry. Anatomy will give you an understanding of the human body, and chemistry will give you insight into the products you will be using. If your school offers drama classes, be sure to take these. Computer classes will give you exposure to this technology, which you may use in the future to create designs. Finally, because this work is typically done on a freelance basis and you will need to manage your business accounts, it will be helpful for you to take math, business, and accounting classes.

You should also try experimenting with makeup on your own. Have professional photographs taken of your efforts to help you begin building a portfolio of your work.

Postsecondary Training

There are a number of postsecondary educational routes you can take to become a makeup artist. If you have experience and a portfolio to show off your work, you may be able to enter the business right out of high school. This route is not always advisable, however, because your chances for establishing a successful freelance career without further training are slim. You must be very ambitious, enthusiastic, and capable of seeking out successful mentors willing to teach you the ropes. This can mean a lot of time working for free or for very little pay.

Another route you can take is to get specific training for makeup artistry through vocational schools. One advantage of this route is that after graduating from the program, you will be able to use the school's career services office, instructors, and other graduates as possible networking sources for jobs.

A third route you can take is to get a broad-based college or university education that results in either a bachelor's or master's degree. Popular majors for makeup artists include theater, art history, film history, photography, and fashion merchandising. In addition to makeup courses, it is important to take classes in painting, illustration, computer design, and animation. A master of fine arts degree in theater or filmmaking will allow you to gain hands-on experience in production as well as working with a faculty of practicing artists.

In addition to formal education, makeup artists need to continue to learn about new styles, techniques, and products throughout their careers. They might attend seminars offered by cosmetics companies, read high fashion magazines, and attend runway shows to stay ahead of the trends.

Other Requirements

Patience and the ability to get along well with people are important for a makeup artist. Throughout a production, the actors will spend many hours in the makeup chair. Though many models and actors will be easy to work with, you may have to put up with much irritability, as well as overwhelming egos.

Attention to detail is important; you must be quick to spot any makeup problems before a model hits the runway or begins filming. Such responsibilities can be stressful—a whole fashion production team will be relying on you to properly apply makeup that will ⟨...⟩ good on the runway or on film. If your work isn't up to par, the wh⟨...⟩ production will suffer. Work as a makeup artist requires as much cr⟨...⟩ ativity and ingenuity as any task. Because of the tough, competitive nature of the fashion and entertainment industries, makeup artists must be persistent and enthusiastic in their pursuit of work.

As a makeup artist, you may want to consider joining a union. The International Alliance of Theatrical Stage Employees (IATSE) represents workers in theater, film, and television production. Hair stylists, makeup artists, engineers, art directors, and set designers are some of the professionals who belong to the 500 local unions affiliated with IATSE. Union membership is not required of most makeup artists for film and theater, but it can help individuals negotiate better wages, benefits, and working conditions. Theaters in larger cities may require union membership of makeup artists, while smaller, regional theaters across the country are less likely to require membership.

EXPLORING

High school drama departments or local community theaters and fashion shows can provide you with great opportunities to explore the makeup artist's work. Volunteer to assist with makeup during a stage production or a local fashion show and you will learn about the materials and tools of a makeup kit, as well as see your work under stage lights. A high school video production team or film department may also offer you opportunities for makeup experience.

EMPLOYERS

Although makeup artists work in a wide variety of circumstances, from fashion and theater, to television and movies, they usually are self-employed, contracting individual jobs. Theater troupes, touring shows, and amusement parks may hire makeup artists on to their staffs, but in the fashion, film, and television industries, makeup artists usually work on a freelance basis. Large cities and metropolitan areas will provide the majority of jobs for makeup artists, particularly those cities associated with the fashion industry, modeling/talent agencies, thriving theaters, or movie or television studios. Although there may be some jobs in smaller towns, they probably will be mostly along the lines of industrial films, corporate videos, and photographic shoots—not very promising for those who wish to make a living in this line of work. Those who aspire to work exclusively as makeup artists gravitate toward the big cities.

STARTING OUT

You should keep a photographic record of all the work you do for fashion, theater, and film productions, including photos of any drawings you've done for art classes. It's important to have a portfolio to send along with your resume to makeup departments, fashion coordinators, and producers. To build up a portfolio of photographs, offer to do makeup for local photographers on a "trade for print" basis. Check with local TV studios about work in their makeup departments. Locally produced newscasts, children's programming, documentaries, and commercials offer opportunities for makeup artists. Commercials are often quick productions (between one and three days) with small casts, and they pay well. Department stores hire makeup artists to demonstrate and sell cosmetic products in department stores, which may be a starting position for those who want to earn a salary while getting on-the-job training and practice.

Because of the freelance nature of the business, you'll be going from project to project. This requires you to constantly seek out work. Read industry trade magazines, and don't be shy about submitting your portfolio to fashion coordinators, producers, and studios. Self-promotion will be an important part of your success as a makeup artist.

ADVANCEMENT

Many makeup artists start as assistants or volunteers on a production, making contacts and connections. They eventually take on projects for which they are in charge of makeup departments and designing makeup effects.

Successful, experienced makeup artists can pick and choose their projects and work as much as they like. In the early years, makeup artists must frequently take on a variety of different projects just for the money; however, as they become established in the field and develop a solid reputation, they can concentrate on projects specific to their interests.

EARNINGS

Makeup artists usually contract with a production, negotiating a daily rate. This rate can vary greatly from project to project, depending on the budget of the production, the prestige of the project, and other factors. Even well-established makeup artists occasionally forgo payment to work on the low-budget independent productions of fashion designers or filmmakers they respect.

Independent contractors don't draw steady, yearly salaries. This means they may work long hours for several weeks, then, upon completion of a production, go without work for several weeks. Unless makeup artists are part of the union, they may be without benefits, having to provide all their own health insurance. An experienced makeup artist can make around $500 a day on a film with a sizable budget with assistants making around $200; some of the top makeup artists in the business command several thousand dollars each day. Theatrical makeup artists can make comparable daily wages on Broadway, or in a theater in a large city; some small theaters, however, may only pay around $50 a day. Day rates for makeup artists in the fashion industry may range from $150 to $800.

Because of such variables as the unsteady nature of the work, the makeup artist's experience, and even where he or she works, the yearly incomes for these individuals vary widely. Some makeup artists may show yearly earnings little higher than those resulting from the minimum wage. Others may have annual income in the hundreds of thousands of dollars. The U.S. Department of Labor reports that makeup artists, theatrical and performance, had median annual salaries of $24,410 in 2004. Salaries ranged from less than $13,410 to more than $63,640. However, celebrity artists can earn salaries of more than $100,000 annually.

WORK ENVIRONMENT

Long hours, deadlines, and tight budgets can create high stress in nearly any production a makeup artist is involved. Because makeup artists move from fashion shoot to theatre production to movie set, they work with different groups of people all the time, and in different locales and settings. Although this allows makeup artists the opportunity to travel, it may also make a makeup artist feel displaced. While working on a production, they may have to forgo a social life, working long hours to design effects and prepare the models and actors. Production workdays can be twice as long as in the average workplace, and those work hours may be a stressful combination of working hurriedly then waiting. For those passionate about the work, however, any uncomfortable or frustrating conditions are easily overlooked.

OUTLOOK

Makeup artists will find their opportunities increasing in the fashion, film, and television industries. The fashion industry continues to grow in popularity, and there will be a continuing need for makeup artists in still photography to prepare models for catalog and magazine shoots. Digital TV has made it possible for hundreds of cable channels to be piped into our homes. The original programming needed to fill the schedules of these new channels results in jobs for makeup artists. Makeup effects artists will find challenging and well-paying work as the film industry pushes the envelope on special effects. These makeup artists may be using computers more and more, as digital design becomes an important tool in creating film effects.

Funding for theaters, some of which comes from the National Endowment for the Arts, is always limited and may be reduced during economic downturns or when productions are unpopular. During these times many theaters may be unable to hire the cast and crew needed for new productions. There has been a revived interest in Broadway, however, due to highly successful musicals like *Rent* and *The Lion King*. This interest could result in better business for traveling productions, as well as regional theaters across the country.

FOR MORE INFORMATION

For information on IATSE, a union representing more than 100,000 members in entertainment and related fields in the United States and Canada, contact
International Alliance of Theatrical Stage Employees (IATSE)
1430 Broadway, 20th Floor
New York, NY 10018
Tel: 212-730-1770
http://www.iatse-intl.org

For information about theater jobs and a sample copy of ArtSEARCH, contact
Theatre Communications Group
520 Eighth Avenue, 24th Floor
New York, NY 10018-4156
Tel: 212-609-5900
Email: tcg@tcg.org
http://www.tcg.org

For information about the Joe Blasco schools and careers in makeup artistry, check out the following website:
Joe Blasco Makeup Training and Cosmetics
http://www.joeblasco.com

Models

OVERVIEW

Models display a wide variety of products and services in print, online, television, and live marketing. *Industrial models* are used in all advertising media to sell every kind of product or service imaginable. *Fashion models* display clothing and fashion accessories in fashion shows, apparel catalogs, and retail stores. A small segment of the modeling field is devoted to posing for commercial and fine artists.

The U.S. Department of Labor classifies models with other workers in occupations bearing on personal appearance. Also in this group are *product demonstrators* and *product promoters*. Of the 179,000 people working in these three fields in the United States, only about 4,600 work as models.

HISTORY

As long as there have been artists, there have been models who posed for them. In earlier times, many of these models were the friends or relatives of the artist. Wealthy patrons also posed for artists to have their portraits painted. Actresses, actors, society personalities, and other celebrities were among the first models.

In 1858, Charles Frederick Worth, an English tailor, opened a salon, or fashion house, in Paris and became the first dressmaker to display his designs on live models.

The history of the photographic model is comparatively recent. Although George Eastman invented the modern camera in 1889, its possible uses in commercial advertising were not realized for more than 20 years. Shortly after the turn of the century, when the ready-to-wear clothing industry began to grow rapidly, businesses discovered

QUIC

School Subjects
Art
Theater/dance

Personal Skills
Artistic
Following instructions

Work Environment
Indoors and outdoors
Primarily multiple locations

Minimum Education Level
High school diploma

Salary Range
$13,790 to $40,000 to
$1 million

Certification or Licensing
None available

Outlook
About as fast as the average

DOT
297

GOE
01.09.01

NOC
5232

O*NET-SOC
41-9011.00, 41-9012.00

that a picture could sell more products than text, and fashion professionals realized that live models boosted clothing sales more than mannequins. Consequently, advertisements began to feature pictures of young women who seemed to endorse a manufacturer's product. As commercial photography continued to grow and develop, so did the career of the photographic model. Today these models can be male or female and of every age, race, and color, depending on the wishes of the advertiser.

The story of fashion models begins in Paris, where they were first employed more than a century ago to display the exclusive clothing designed by French dressmakers for wealthy women. Before 1900, U.S. fashions were, for the most part, copies of the French originals, and it was seldom considered necessary for copied clothing to be shown by live models. Shortly after World War I, the U.S. garment industry created some original designs. These garments were mass produced. As these fashion houses slowly multiplied, so did the number of models needed to show new clothing designs to prospective buyers. In the past 40 years, the U.S. garment industry has assumed world leadership in the production of clothing, and increasing numbers of models have been needed to display these garments and the fashion accessories that go with them.

THE JOB

Models are generally grouped according to the medium or media in which they work. For instance, models who perform with movement in fashion shows and for retail stores (on the floor) are known as fashion models. Those who pose for artists are known as *artists' models,* and those who advertise products and services in print are known as *photographic models*. In large cities there are modeling agencies that specialize in handling petite, plus-size, specialty, character, beauty, photographic, and high fashion models.

The work of artists' models is to pose for an individual artist or for a class of art students. When posing, models must stand or sit in one position for several hours at a time. A quick break for relaxation is usually given once each hour. Often the model must pose on a platform under hot and bright lights and sometimes wear little or no clothing. One job may last a day, while another may last for several weeks.

Photographic models pose for photographs. Their job is to lend attractiveness to an advertisement and enhance the desirability of the product. These models encounter a great variety of situations in their work. One series of photographs may be taken in a studio under hot lights with the model wearing a heavy fur coat. Another may be taken outdoors in midwinter with the model wearing only a bathing suit. One job may last only an hour, while another may require an entire day. In their work, models may travel to other states or even to other countries to be photographed in beautiful, unusual, or exotic settings.

Rarely do photographic models work full time. Days or weeks may pass between one job and the next, especially if they work on a freelance basis. If models contract with a modeling agency, however, their schedule may be fuller because the agency will be able to secure modeling jobs for them.

The photographic model who has some acting ability may secure a job in a television commercial. These ads are usually videotaped or filmed. Although television modeling is very lucrative, it is very difficult for the average model to break into this field, mainly due to lack of training in acting.

Specialty models must possess particular features that are photogenic, such as hands, feet, legs, hair, lips, or ears that will help sell specific products.

Fashion models differ from the other types of models in three basic ways. First, the models usually work for clothing manufacturers, fashion designers, or department stores on a full-time basis. Second, they do not merely pose in one position, but walk around and assume a variety of poses in their display of the clothing. Third, they often speak to prospective purchasers to inform them of the model number and price of each garment.

Some fashion models may be employed by clothing manufacturers as showroom and fitting models. In many large department stores, a staff of full-time models is employed to promote the sale of various garments or accessories. The store may have a regularly scheduled style show during the daily lunch hour; at other times, models may walk throughout the store showing apparel and talking with customers about the garments and accessories being worn. Those models hired by a distributor to hand out free product samples, such as perfume or food, are known as *sampling demonstration models* or *product promoters*.

All fashion models employ certain techniques to display their clothing in the most effective way. Good grooming is basic for most models, from the proper application of makeup and hair care to the smallest personal details. Models must walk gracefully with an erect carriage and master the techniques of pivoting to show the sides and back of a garment. They must know how to carry their hands and arms gracefully, as well as the body positions needed to emphasize certain details of their costume. They also must be able to call attention to accessories, such as purses, jewelry, and gloves.

Some fashion models do not work regularly but are called only for special style shows or certain buyers' showings. Some prefer to freelance since they may have other jobs or responsibilities. The most successful models work in all areas of the field, from live fashion modeling to print work to video and film modeling, as well as acting and live industrial and promotional presentations.

REQUIREMENTS

High School
There are no standard educational requirements for models. Most employers of photographic models prefer at least a high school education. Courses such as sewing, home economics, and photography are helpful. Classes in dance, fencing, Tai Chi, and other disciplines that focus on body and movement control provide a good foundation for modeling. Public speaking and business courses are helpful since models often work as freelancers.

Postsecondary Training
Many employers of models state a preference for college graduates with the ability to communicate well and with a general cultural background. Academic courses may include art, drama, art history, photography, history, English, speech, or debate. Some models take special courses in sports or physical fitness, such as dance, swimming, skiing, skating, aerobics, or horseback riding to get into and stay in shape and develop physical coordination, suppleness, and grace. As models often keep track of their own expenses, a basic knowledge of bookkeeping and mathematics also is helpful.

Other Requirements
There are significant differences in the requirements necessary for each type of model. The major requirement for the fashion model is, of course, physical appearance. Although most people think of all models as being young and slender, that is not necessarily the case. No set standard exists for a model's physical description because many different body types are needed. Many garment manufacturers seek female fashion models who are between the ages of 16 and 30, between 5 feet 8 inches and 5 feet 11 inches in height and wear from a size six to a size 10. Male models generally must be between 6 feet and 6 feet 2 inches in height and wear a size 40 or 42 regular suit. People who fail to meet these specifications, however, should

A model displays the
newest in men's fashion
on a runway. *(Corbis)*

not feel that there are no possibilities for them in this career; after
all, garments and other fashion items are made for people of all sizes
and types. Also, atypical models who do not necessarily possess classical model features, proportions, or body types, but display interesting or unusual personal style, increasingly are being seen on runways
and in photo advertisements, reflecting designer, commercial, and
public acceptance of cultural and physical diversity and individual
expression in fashion.

Because some fashion houses create styles for people of middle
years whose weight is closer to average, more mature looking models sometimes are needed. Other firms that specialize in evening
clothes often require models of above average height to display their
garments. Companies that produce junior sizes require models who

Books to Read

Matheson, Eve. *The Modeling Handbook.* 4th ed. Boca Raton, Fla.: Peter Glenn Publications, 2000.

McKinney, Anne, ed. *Real-Resumes for Retailing, Modeling, Fashion and Beauty Industry Jobs: Including Real Resumes Used to Change Careers and Transfer Skills to Other Industries.* Fayetteville, N.C.: Prep Publishing, 2002.

Model & Talent Directory: International Directory of Model and Talent Agencies and Schools. Boca Raton, Fla.: Peter Glenn Publications, 2004. Moellers, Marcia Rothschild. *So, You Want to Be a Fashion Model?* New York: Interscout, LLC, 2003.

Press, Debbie. *Your Modeling Career.* New York: Allworth Press, 2004.

Rose, Yvonne, and Tony Rose. *Is Modeling for You?: The Handbook and Guide for the Young Aspiring Black Model.* Phoenix, Ariz.: Amber Books, 1998.

can wear those sizes without alterations. Those that manufacture misses' or women's sizes may seek models who can wear sizes eight, 10, or 12. They also may seek full-figured models who wear sizes 14 or larger. Petite models are 5 feet 5 inches and wear uneven sizes such as three, five, and seven.

The basic requirement for photographers' models is that they photograph well. It must be emphasized, however, that not all attractive people have the qualities that commercial photographers require. Many times characteristics such as wholesomeness and sincerity, as well as freshness of face or manner, are as important in this field as good looks.

Modeling is a particularly fatiguing occupation because it requires many hours of standing and walking, or sitting or standing still in uncomfortable positions. Thus, good health and physical stamina are important. In addition, those people interested in being fashion or photographic models must be prepared to give up most of their social life and limit their diets. To maintain their figures and appearances, they will require many extra hours of sleep each night and will need to avoid rich foods and beverages.

Another important requirement is immaculate grooming. Fashion and photographic models will have to spend more hours than the average person taking care of their skin, hair, nails, and general physical fitness. Especially important to fashion models is the ability to walk gracefully while carrying their hands, arms, and torso in a poised and chic manner.

Most fashion and photographers' models must have special training to meet all of the above requirements. Entering a reputable modeling school to learn the skills and techniques of modeling or enrolling in a good charm school to learn makeup application, appropriate clothing, and the proper ways to walk and stand are also helpful and can be a shortcut into the business.

EXPLORING

If you are an aspiring model, you should read about the modeling industry and contact modeling agencies to gain an understanding of what their needs may include. Experience in fashion modeling may be obtained in home economics courses as well as from local fashion shows. Many fashion design schools stage fashion shows for their students' designs and need amateur models to donate their time.

You may want to talk with the buyer or fashion director of a large local store or seek the advice of a commercial photographer, who often help new talent get started, about your opportunities for a successful modeling career and the special areas for which you may be qualified. Modeling agencies also may be approached for their opinions. It is important to assess your chances for meaningful work before moving to a big city or investing in expensive modeling classes, photographs, and wardrobe.

EMPLOYERS

The approximately 4,600 models employed in the United States work in a variety of settings that require different skills and qualifications. Fashion models may be employed by apparel firms or retail stores; photographic models work through one or more agencies for a variety of clients. High fashion models usually work in major fashion centers such as New York, London, or Paris. Large cities generally offer more opportunities for modeling work than small towns.

A large percentage of those in the modeling industry do not work full time as models, since there are far more applicants than assignments. Therefore many models have other means of supporting themselves. Models generally choose part-time jobs, especially those with flexible schedules or evening work, in order to be available for auditions and assignments. Many work as restaurant servers, though individuals with special skills or training may find other work. Some work in sales, which allows them flexibility in schedules and number of hours.

STARTING OUT

To gain employment as an artist's model, men or women may apply directly at various art schools, cautiously check newspaper want ads, or apply at the state employment office.

Graduates of modeling schools may be aided by school career services offices when securing their first job. Another possibility for the prospective model is to register at a modeling agency. Aspiring models, however, should be wary of disreputable agencies or schools that promise jobs for a fee toward the purchase of a portfolio of photographs or a contract for modeling classes. Legitimate agencies and modeling schools are listed in industry publications. Choose a modeling agency certified by such bodies as the Screen Actors Guild (SAG) or check with your local Better Business Bureau or Chamber of Commerce to make sure the agency or school is licensed by the state education department before signing an agreement or paying money to an agency or service that promises jobs.

Many agencies select only those people with qualities they feel will be demanded by their clients. If accepted by an agency, the future model's composite card and photographs are placed on file and the model will be called for a job when the agency feels they have one for which the person is qualified. In return for the agency's services, models pay 15 to 20 percent of their earnings to the agency.

All models who wish to have a career in modeling are required to have a collection of photographs to show prospective employers. These photographs should include at least one head shot and several full-length shots in various kinds of situations and garments to show the model's versatility and ability to sell whatever he or she is modeling. Photographic models must have multiple copies of these photographs to leave with potential employers. The back of each picture should list the model's name, address, a contact phone number, height, weight, and coloring, along with clothing and shoe sizes. This picture will be placed in a file along with pictures of many other models. When someone of this type and size is needed for a picture, the model may be called to pose. Models include tear sheets in their portfolios from the assignments they have completed. These sheets prove to prospective employers the model's experience and ability.

Aspiring models who plan to seek work in a large, unfamiliar city should go there prepared to look for a job for at least three months. They should have enough money to support themselves and pay for such modeling necessities as a fashionable wardrobe, professional hair and beauty care, adequate diet, and such incidentals as additional photographs or special short-term training.

ADVANCEMENT

The modeling profession has no standard line o[...]
rare for artists' models to advance in the usua[...]
It is to be expected, however, that the better [...]
more successful artists may pay higher hourly v[...]
models.

Advancement for fashion or photographic models takes the form
of increased income and greater demand for their talent. However,
their careers usually are short. The model who works in the field for
longer than eight years is considered highly unusual. Certain physical changes and lifestyle often make it difficult for older people to
compete with younger models for the same type of assignments.

Even a high degree of success can lead to the shortening of a
model's career. When models appear too frequently on magazine
covers or in features, the uniqueness of their look becomes familiar,
and they are passed by in favor of models who have not received
such wide coverage. Also, models who become identified with one
particular product, such as a line of makeup or shampoo, may find
it difficult to qualify for jobs with other employers.

Most fashion and photographic models must therefore learn a
marketable skill or profession to which they may turn when they
can no longer continue modeling. Many fashion models gain enough
knowledge to move into fashion design, advertising, public relations, or retailing. Others attend special schools between modeling
assignments to learn business, technical, or vocational skills. Still
others go to work for modeling agencies or open agencies of their
own. Modeling can be a gateway to consulting jobs in the fashion
and merchandising field, and some models serve as board members
of fashion magazines. Other models become actors and actresses.
Well-known models may develop their own line of cosmetics or
other products.

EARNINGS

Earnings for models vary according to experience and depend on the
number, length, and type of assignments he or she receives. Today,
top fashion models working full time for wholesalers or retailers earn
approximately $40,000 or more a year. Models working retail shows
earn between $15,000 and $18,000 or more each year. Female models working for agencies make $100 to $125 an hour. Hourly wages
are higher for photographic models working in large metropolitan
cities such as New York, Miami, Los Angeles, or Chicago and for

who are in great demand. Top photographic models signed xclusive contracts with cosmetic firms may earn $1 million or ore per year. Almost all models work with agents and pay 15 to 20 percent of their earnings in return for an agent's services.

The *Occupational Outlook Handbook* reports that median hourly earnings of models were $10.09 in 2004. The lowest 10 percent earned less than $6.63, and the highest 10 percent earned more than $17.18.

Models who appear in television commercials are paid according to the fee schedules set up by the two major unions, the Screen Actors Guild (SAG) and the American Federation of Television and Radio Artists (AFTRA). Models who speak earn more than those who do not. In addition, they receive a fee called a residual whenever the commercial is aired.

Fashion models who are employed by department stores are called *floor models*. They work only for special promotions at the store and earn the same salary as salespeople. The rate of pay is generally between $8 and $12 an hour, depending on the size and location of the store and the quality and cost of the merchandise. Models who work for advertising agencies may earn between $15 and $25 an hour. The more versatile the model, the greater the opportunity for employment.

Because they are seldom employed full time, instead earning a high hourly fee on an occasional basis, photographic models may not always have enough money to maintain themselves between jobs. They may find it necessary to seek other kinds of work on a temporary basis. Because it is essential that they have outstanding wardrobes, they frequently work at part-time jobs to buy the necessary clothes for their assignments. Models occasionally receive clothing or clothing discounts instead of, or in addition to, regular earnings.

The only full-time employment for models usually is as a spokesperson for a store or company. Full-time models usually receive up to two or three weeks of vacation per year. The perks of being a fashion model include the chance to wear beautiful clothes, look your best, and be groomed by photographers, designers, artists, and hair and makeup professionals. Some models travel to exciting places and meet interesting and famous people; a very few may even attain celebrity status. Indeed, today's fashion and cosmetics supermodels have achieved a celebrity status that formerly was the exclusive domain of movie stars. Historically, the industry favors youth, but older models now are being used by agencies more often and the age barrier seems to be coming down. Young people who hope to become models, however, should approach the career with the understanding that competition is keen and that it may take years of work to attain success. But even the beginner, on a local level, can make enough money to make this career worthwhile.

WORK ENVIRONMENT

Modeling can be exciting, challenging, glamorous, and rewarding, but also very stressful. Modeling is not a routine job and to be successful, models must have the drive, patience, and self-confidence to adjust and meet new challenges. They also must be able to accept rejection, since many assignments require auditions where many qualified applicants compete.

Models work under a variety of conditions. The artist's model usually works indoors in a loft, a studio, or a classroom. These rooms may be large and drafty with high ceilings and inadequate heating or cooling facilities. The more modern art schools, however, will be comfortably heated, ventilated, and lighted. This model may pose in ordinary street clothing, in exotic costumes, or in body-revealing attire.

Photographic models may work either indoors or outdoors. There may be times when models are asked to pose in bathing suits while standing outside in chilly weather. At other times, they may model wool clothing in midsummer on hot city pavements. In photographers' studios, models often are asked to hold a pose for a long period of time while lights and background details are adjusted. Models need patience to wait while problems are solved and many different people offer opinions about any one shot.

Many agency models must carry heavy bags of cosmetics, grooming tools, accessories, and garments as they travel from one client to another.

Fashion models usually work indoors in comfortable showrooms, hotels, or restaurants. They must stand and walk a great deal during busy seasons. During slack seasons, there may be little for runway and showroom models to do and time may pass slowly. If they are employed in a department store, models are able to walk about the store and talk with customers. Although they are on their feet for most of the working day, they enjoy a variety of settings and people in their work. Models must enjoy their work thoroughly and not allow themselves to become impatient or exasperated by rejection, delays, or disappointments. Many young persons who enter a modeling career do so because they anticipate that it will be glamorous. Once embarked upon the career, they find little glamour and much hard work. Nevertheless, there are many satisfactions to be found in achieving success in this demanding field. Most models enjoy dressing well and looking trim and fit. They enjoy the excitement of the fashion and advertising worlds. They may find that the people with whom they work are interesting and may have an opportunity to meet or to work with famous or successful persons. Although their careers as models may be short, often they have a worthwhile second career in fashion, advertising, business, or public relations.

OUTLOOK

The U.S. Department of Labor predicts employment for models to grow about as fast as the average through 2012, but job competition will be fierce because this career is attractive to so many people. The number of fashion models seeking jobs is far greater than the number of openings. A greater number of openings exist for artists' models, but their income almost never is enough to live on. Part-time work is easier to find than full-time work. The number of models working should increase as the economy becomes more global. Models from the United States are in demand around the world. Opportunities for male models should also increase as the public becomes more open to the marketing of men's fashions. Most openings will occur as models quit or retire to pursue other employment or interests.

FOR MORE INFORMATION

It is suggested that aspiring models gather information from a variety of sources: agencies, books, and articles. Little information is available to help students in their choices other than checking schools and agencies with the local Better Business Bureau or Chamber of Commerce and talking with experienced models. The SAG and the AFTRA do not represent models unless they become actors.

This is an organization of training centers for models and talent. Visit its website for information on modeling careers, competitions, and annual conventions.
 International Modeling and Talent Association
 http://www.imta.com

For advice on becoming a model, visit the following websites:
 E-MODEL.NET
 http://www.e-model.net

Modeling Advice
http://www.modelingadvice.com

For information about the modeling industry and a listing of modeling agencies in the United States and abroad, visit the following website:
The Insider's Guide to Supermodels and Modeling
http://www.supermodelguide.com

Visit the following website for advice on avoiding modeling scams:
Modeling Scams
http://www.modelingscams.org

To read about fashions, models, and agencies, check out the following website:
Models.com
http://models.com

Nail Technicians

QUICK FACTS

School Subjects
Art
Business
Health

Personal Skills
Artistic
Helping/teaching

Work Environment
Primarily indoors
Primarily one location

Minimum Education Level
Some postsecondary training

Salary Range
$15,232 to $18,130 to
$22,000+

Certification or Licensing
Required by certain states

Outlook
Faster than the average

DOT
331

GOE
11.04.01

NOC
6482

O*NET-SOC
39-5092.00

OVERVIEW

Nail technicians clean, shape, and polish fingernails and toenails. They groom cuticles and apply cream to hands and arms (feet and calves in the case of pedicures). They apply a variety of artificial nails and provide ongoing maintenance. Many nail technicians are skilled in "nail art" and decorate clients' nails with stencils, glitter, and ornaments. Nail technicians may also call themselves *manicurists, pedicurists, nail sculpturists,* or *nail artists.* There are approximately 51,000 nail technicians working in the United States.

HISTORY

The word *manicure* comes from the Latin *manus* (hand) and *cura* (care). In ancient times, dramatically long and decorated fingernails were a mark of wealth and status, clearly distinguishing an aristocrat from a laborer. Historical artifacts reveal that the practice of caring for and decorating the fingernails dates back thousands of years. The excavation of one Assyrian tomb uncovered a 5,000-year-old cuticle stick. The ancient Egyptians used henna to stain their nails, and cosmetic kits have been discovered even in the tombs of Egyptian women, who took with them everything they might need in the next world.

Makeup remained in fashion throughout the Renaissance, although the Western ideal for fingernails was a natural look. Women took great pains to have soft, beautiful hands. They slept in gloves made from thin leather, lined with almond paste and oil from sperm whales. During this time, the Eastern habit of dyeing the nails and hands continued. Lady Mary Wortley Montague, an upper-class Englishwoman, wrote in 1717 of this practice, "I own I cannot enough accustom my selfe [sic] to this fashion to find any Beauty in it." Men and women alike were held to high standards for grooming of the hands during this time, as is evidenced in an 18th-century letter from the Earl of Chesterfield to his son: "Nothing looks more ordinary, vulgar, and illiberal, than dirty hands and ugly, uneven, ragged nails."

Predictably, the Victorian era frowned upon makeup. Decorative makeup was the mark of a loose woman, so the style for fingernails was au natural. The end of the 19th century marked the advent of a change in this sentiment, when "nail powders" began to be advertised in Paris. Then, in 1907, liquid nail polish was introduced, the polish lightly tinted with rose dyes. For women who were wary of this new product, solid or powdered nail rouges were available. Nail kits containing files, orange sticks, cuticle implements, and so forth became popular in the first decade of the 20th century. The use of makeup was now becoming acceptable. *Vogue* asserted in 1920, "Even the most conservative and prejudiced people now concede that a woman exquisitely made up may yet be, in spite of seeming frivolity, a faithful wife and devoted mother."

Once the acceptability of makeup was established, a myriad of styles abounded in the 20th century. The year 1930 brought the invention of opaque nail polish as we know it today. Blood-red nails quickly became the rage, although the trendsetting Parisian women were soon sporting green, blue, white, and even black nails to match their clothing ensembles and jewels, sometimes even adding shocking decorative touches not unlike the handiwork of modern-day nail artists.

Also in 1930, *Harper's Bazaar* introduced the idea that fashionable women should match their nail polish and their lipstick. New colors began to flourish in the 1930s, including corals, pinks, and beiges. The 1940s brought yet more naturalistic colors in makeup. In America, Hollywood played a significant role in pushing makeup into the realm of the glamorous. Production of makeup slowed down during World War II as supplies became scarce. But the makeup frenzy exploded in the 1950s when the marketing geniuses at Revlon dictated that colors should change with the season, and women scrambled to get their hands on each new shade as it was introduced. It was also during the 1950s that a dentist in Philadelphia invented sculptured nails, which were quickly embraced and promoted by celebrities such as Cher and Tina Sinatra. Long, fashionable nails were now within the reach of all women.

Elizabeth Taylor's *Cleopatra* inspired the dramatic, dark-eyed look of the early 1960s, and the eyes continued to dominate the

Industry Stats, 2005

- The average nail technician has been on the job for 9.1 years.
- Nearly 95 percent of nail technicians are licensed.
- Nearly 96 percent of nail technicians are women.
- Thirty-one percent of nail technicians have a high school diploma.
- Nearly 16 percent have finished college, and 4.2 percent have a graduate degree.

Source: *NAILS Magazine*

makeup scene into the 1970s, while lips and nails faded into the background. However, by 1972, wild nail colors were once again in full swing, and Revlon introduced a line called "Lady in the Dark," whose 24 shades included variations of green, purple, blue, and black. Of course, with the concurrent advent of the back-to-nature movement in the 1970s, not every women rushed out to buy the latest shade. A truly natural approach to self-care was also developing, which has been largely synthesized into the concepts and products of the last two decades.

Today, both decorative and natural makeup styles have an established place, and there are fingernail products and styles to suit everyone. While many nail products (including artificial nail kits) continue to be widely available at the retail level, more and more women—and men—are seeking out the services of professional nail technicians.

THE JOB

Nail technicians generally work at a manicurist table and chair or stool across from their clients. Their work implements include finger bowls, electric heaters, wet sanitizer containers, alcohol, nail sticks and files, cuticle instruments, emery boards and buffers, tweezers, nail polishes and removers, abrasives, creams and oils, and nail dryers.

Standard manicure procedure involves removing old polish, shaping nails, softening and trimming cuticles and applying cuticle cream, cleansing and drying hands and nails, applying polish and top coat, and applying hand lotion. As an extra service, lotion is often massaged into the wrists and arms as well as the hands. Technicians should always follow a sanitary cleanup procedure at their stations following each manicure, including sanitizing instruments and table, discarding used materials, and washing and drying their hands.

A man's manicure is a more conservative procedure than a woman's; the process is similar, but most men prefer to have a dry polish or to have their nails buffed.

Pedicuring has become a popular and important salon service, especially when fashion and weather dictate open-toed shoe styles. The procedure for a pedicure is much like that of a manicure, with the set-up involving a low stool for the technician and an ottoman for the client's feet.

Nail technicians also provide other services, including the application of artificial nails. A number of techniques are employed, depending on the individual client's preferences and nail characteristics. These include nail wrapping, nail sculpturing, nail tipping, press-on nails, and nail dipping. Technicians also repair broken nails and do "fill-ins" on artificial nails as the real nails grow out.

Nail technicians must take care to use only new or sanitized instruments to prevent the spread of disease. The rapid growth of this industry has been accompanied by an increased awareness of the many ways in which viral, fungal, and bacterial infections can be spread. Many states have passed laws regarding the use of various instruments. Although nail technicians may be exposed to such contagious diseases as athlete's foot and ringworm, the use of gloves is not a practical solution due to the level of precision required in a nail technician's work. For this reason, nail technicians must be able to distinguish between skin or nail conditions that can be treated in the salon and disorders and diseases that require medical attention. In so doing, educated and honest nail technicians can contribute to the confidence, health, and well-being of their customers.

REQUIREMENTS

High School

Many states require that nail technicians be high school graduates, although a few states require only an eighth- or 10th-grade education. If you are interested in becoming a nail technician, consider taking health and anatomy classes in high school. These classes will give you a basis for understanding skin and nail conditions. Since many nail technicians are self-employed, you may benefit from taking business classes that teach you how a successful business is run. Take art classes, such as painting, drawing, or sculpting, that will allow you to work with your hands and develop a sense of color and design. Finally, don't forget to take English or communication classes. These courses will help you hone your speaking and writing skills, skills that you will need when dealing with the public. Some high schools with vocational programs may offer cosmetology courses. Such courses may include the study of bacteriology, sanitation, and mathematics. These specialized courses can be helpful in preparing students for their future work. You will need to check with your high school about the availability of such a vocational program.

Postsecondary Training

Your next step on the road to becoming a nail technician is to attend a cosmetology or nail school. Some states have schools specifically for nail technician training; in other states, the course work must be completed within the context of a full cosmetology program. Nail technology courses generally require between 100 and 500 clock hours of training, but requirements can vary widely from state to state. Because of these variations, make sure the school you choose to attend will allow you to meet the educational requirements of the state in which you hope to work. When the required course work has been completed, you must pass an examination that usually includes a written test and a practical examination to demonstrate mastery of required skills. A health certificate is sometimes required.

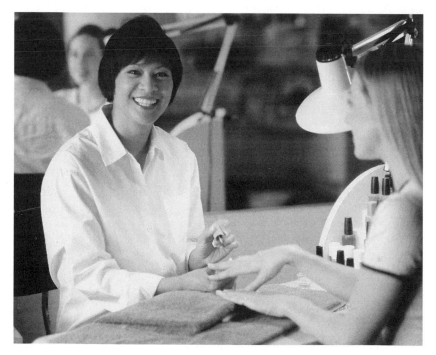

Nail technicians must have good vision and manual dexterity, as their work is very exacting in nature. *(Corbis)*

Course work in nail schools (or nail technician programs in cosmetology schools) reflects that students are expected to learn a great deal more than just manicuring; typical courses of study encompass a broad array of subjects. The course outline at Pivot Point International (with affiliated schools throughout the United States) includes bacteriology, sanitation, and aseptic control procedures; diseases and disorders of the nail; anatomy (of the nails, hands, and feet); nail styling and artificial nail techniques; spa manicures and pedicures; aromatherapy; reflexology; state law; advertising and sales; and people skills. Course work also includes working on live models so that each student graduates with hands-on experience in each service studied.

Certification or Licensing

Most states require nail technicians to be licensed. Usually a fee is charged to take the exam, and another fee is assessed before receiving the license. Exams usually include both written and practical tests. Many states now offer special nail technician licenses (sometimes called limited or specialty certificates), which require anywhere from 100 to 500 hours of schooling in a licensed cosmetology or nail school. In states where no limited certificates are offered, a student must complete cosmetology school (substantially more hours than required for a specialty), become licensed as a cosmetologist, and then specialize in nail technology. Some states offer special licenses for manicurist managers and nail technician instructors; these require substantially more hours of schooling than do nail technician licenses. Reciprocity agreements exist in some states that enable a nail technician to work in another state without being retested. Some states require that nail technicians be 16 or 18 years old in order to be licensed. You will need to find out the licensing requirements for the state in which you hope to work. Associations and state boards of health can often supply this information.

Other Requirements

Nail technicians must have good vision and manual dexterity, as their work is very exacting in nature. Creativity and artistic talents are helpful, especially for those technicians who perform nail art, which can include painting designs and applying various decorative items to nails. A steady hand is important, and nail technicians should also have an eye for form and color.

Since nail technicians provide services to a wide variety of people, the personality and attitude of a nail technician to a large extent ultimately determine his or her success. While some clients are easy to please, others are demanding and even unreasonable; a nail technician who is able to satisfy even the most difficult customers will be positioned to develop a large, loyal following. Nail technicians who are punctual, courteous, respectful, and patient will enjoy a distinct competitive advantage over others in the industry who lack these qualities. Tact, professionalism, and competence are important. Knowledge and practice of proper sanitizing techniques should be clearly visible to clients. Naturally, hygiene and grooming are of paramount importance in this profession, and a nail technician's own hands and nails should be perfectly groomed; this is one's best form of advertisement and can help foster confidence in prospective and new clients.

A confident, outgoing personality can be a great boon to a nail technician's success. Customers may readily accept recommendations for additional nail services from a persuasive, knowledgeable, and competent nail technician who appears genuinely interested in the customer's interests. Nail technicians who can successfully sell their services will enjoy increased business.

Unlike most careers in the cosmetology field, nail technicians are not required to be on their feet all day. Nail technology is a good choice for those interested in the beauty industry who prefer to be able to work in a seated, comfortable position.

EXPLORING

If you are considering a career as a nail technician, a good avenue of exploration is to call a cosmetology or nail school and ask for an opportunity to tour the facilities, observe classes, and question instructors. Another enjoyable option is for you to make an appointment with a nail technician for a manicure or pedicure. By receiving one of these services yourself, you will have the opportunity to visit the place of business, take in the atmosphere, and experience the procedure. In addition, you'll have the opportunity to talk to someone who can answer your questions about this line of work. Explain that you are interested in becoming a nail technician, and you may find that you can develop a mentoring relationship with this professional technician. A part-time job in a beauty salon that offers nail services may also help you determine your interest in various aspects of the beauty industry. Part-time positions for nontechnicians in nail salons, though, may prove difficult to find.

EMPLOYERS

As with cosmetologists and other personal appearance workers, approximately half of the nail technicians in the country are self-

Nail Technicians by Ethnicity, 2005

White: 43 percent
Vietnamese: 39 percent
African American: 8 percent
Hispanic: 7 percent
Korean: 2 percent
Asian/other: 1 percent

Source: *NAILS Magazine*

employed. They may rent a "booth" or chair at a salon; some may own their own nail salons. A growing number of nail technicians are employed by nail salons, which are rapidly increasing in number in many areas of the country. Beauty shops and department store salons also employ nail technicians, but most have only one or two on staff (very large salons have more). Since nail services represent one of the fastest-growing segments of the cosmetology industry, there is good potential for those wishing to open their own businesses in the nail industry.

STARTING OUT

In most states, graduating from an accredited cosmetology or nail school that meets the state's requirements for licensing is the vehicle for entry into this field. Nearly all cosmetology schools assist graduates with the process of finding employment. Want ads and personal visits to salons and shops are also productive means of finding a job.

ADVANCEMENT

Advancement in the nail technology industry most often takes the form of establishing a large, loyal clientele. Other opportunities include owning one's own nail salon. This can be a highly profitable endeavor if one has the proper business skills and savvy; the cost of materials and overhead can be relatively low, and, in addition to the earnings realized from services performed for their customers, the owners typically receive half of their operators' earnings.

Some technicians choose to advance by becoming nail instructors in cosmetology or nail schools or becoming inspectors for state cosmetology boards.

Nail technicians who constantly strive to increase their knowledge and proficiency in a wide array of nail services will have a competitive advantage and will be positioned to secure a large and varied clientele.

EARNINGS

Income for nail technicians can vary widely, depending on the skill, experience, and clientele of the nail technician, the type and location of the shop or salon, the tipping habits of the clientele, and the area of the country. The U.S. Department of Labor reports the median annual income for nail technicians was $18,130 in 2004. (This income includes tips.) Salary.com, a provider of compensation information, reports that nationwide manicurists had yearly earnings ranging from approximately less than $15,232 to $18,514 in May 2004. Those working in large metropolitan areas may have slightly higher earnings, but the cost of living is also higher there.

The importance of the talents and personality of the nail technician cannot be underestimated when evaluating potential earnings. Those who hold themselves to the highest levels of professionalism, express a genuine interest in clients' well-being, and provide the highest quality service quickly develop loyal clienteles, and these nail technicians will realize earnings that far exceed the averages.

Those technicians who work in beauty shops are less likely than those in nail salons to have appointments scheduled throughout the day; however, customers in beauty salons often pay more and tip better for these services. Also, there is less competition within the beauty shop setting, as the majority of beauty salons employ only one or two nail technicians.

Owning one's own nail salon can be very profitable, as the cost of equipment is relatively low. In addition to taking home one's own earnings from servicing clients, the owner also generally gets half of the income generated by the shop's other operators. Nail salons are a prime example of a small business with tremendous potential for success.

Except for those nail technicians who work in department stores or large salons, most do not enjoy much in the way of benefits; few nail technicians receive health and life insurance or paid vacations.

WORK ENVIRONMENT

Nail technicians work indoors in bright, well-ventilated, comfortable environments. Unlike most careers in the cosmetology industry that require operators to be on their feet most of the day, nail technicians perform their work seated at a table.

Many nail technicians work five-day weeks including Saturdays, which are a high-volume business day in this industry. Working some evenings may be helpful in building one's clientele, as a large percentage of customers are working professionals. Nail technicians often enjoy some flexibility in their hours, and many enjoy successful part-time careers.

A large number of nail technicians are self-employed; they may rent a space in a beauty or nail salon. Often, nail technicians must provide their own supplies and tools. Nail technicians are exposed to a certain amount of chemicals and dust, but this is generally manageable in well-ventilated work surroundings. Those who work in full-service salons may be exposed to additional chemicals and odors.

Inherent in the nature of a nail technician's work is the constant company of others. A nail technician who is not a "people person" will find this line of work most challenging. But since most people who choose this career enjoy the company of others, they find the opportunity to talk with and get to know people to be one of the most satisfying and enjoyable aspects of their work.

OUTLOOK

The nail business (a multibillion dollar industry) has been growing rapidly for years. Nail salons and day spas offering nail services continue to crop up everywhere, and nail technicians represent the fastest-growing segment of the various specialized service providers in the beauty industry. According to the U.S. Department of Labor, employment for nail technicians should grow faster than the average through 2012.

Once a mark of feminine status, nail services are now sought and enjoyed by a wide variety of people, both male and female. Helen Barkan, whose clients have dubbed her the "Nail Doctor," has been a nail technician and salon owner in the Deerbrook Mall in Deerfield, Illinois, for the past 24 years, and she has been doing nails for more years than she'll reveal. Barkan, whose straightforward services focus on helping clients grow strong, healthy nails (she doesn't do artificial nails), says, "Many of my clients have been coming to me for more than 20 years. I've always been willing to spend a little extra time and go the extra mile for my customers, and at one time I worked seven days a week. My clients are important to me, and they know that." Barkan has watched the industry change dramatically over the decades. Today, approximately one-third of Barkan's customers are men, and they come for manicures and pedicures alike. Clearly, there is a market for all kinds of nail services, from the most basic hand and nail care to the most involved procedures and outlandish styles.

FOR MORE INFORMATION

This magazine has information on the latest nail technologies, fashions, safety matters, and industry news.
NAILS Magazine
3520 Challenger Street
Torrance, CA 90503
Tel: 310-533-2400
Email: nailsmag@nailsmag.com
http://www.nailsmag.com

This organization accredits cosmetology schools nationally and can provide lists of licensed training schools.
National Accrediting Commission of Cosmetology Arts and Sciences
4401 Ford Avenue, Suite 1300
Alexandria, VA 22302
Tel: 703-600-7600
http://www.naccas.org

This organization of nail technicians, stylists, salon owners, and other professionals can provide industry and education information.
National Cosmetology Association
401 North Michigan Avenue, 22nd Floor
Chicago, IL 60611
Tel: 312-527-6765
http://www.salonprofessionals.org

This website for beauty professionals has a list of state licensing requirements for nail technicians.
Beauty Tech
http://www.beautytech.com/nailtech

Shoe Industry Workers

OVERVIEW

Shoe industry workers turn materials such as leather, rubber, fabrics, and plastic into finished shoes, boots, moccasins, sandals, slippers, and other footwear. Most of these workers operate machines. *Shoe and leather repairers* repair and re-style shoes and other products, such as saddles, harnesses, handbags, and luggage. More highly skilled *custom shoemakers* and *orthopedic shoe designers and makers* may design, construct, or repair orthopedic shoes in accordance with foot specialists' prescriptions. Approximately 16,000 shoe and leather workers and repairers work in the United States.

HISTORY

Shoemaking in North America began as a craft in 1629 when London shoemaker Thomas Beard settled in Salem, Massachusetts, to make shoes under contract for the Massachusetts Bay Colony. Later, itinerant colonial cobblers made crude, buckled shoes that could be worn on either foot. Shoemakers set up shops in villages and passed on their trade to apprentices. In 1760, a Welshman named John Adam Dagyr, the father of American shoemaking, began operating the first shoe factory in Lynn, Massachusetts. Under this system, workers specialized in one shoemaking operation.

Until the 18th century, good quality, shaped footwear was made by shoemakers who used essentially the same methods that had been used everywhere since ancient times. Shoemakers were skilled artisans who could take raw materials like leather, wood, thread,

QUICK FACTS

School Subjects
Family and consumer science
Technical/shop

Personal Skills
Following instructions
Mechanical/manipulative

Work Environment
Primarily indoors
Primarily one location

Minimum Education Level
Apprenticeship

Salary Range
$12,000 to $19,780 to
$28,430

Certification or Licensing
None available

Outlook
Decline

DOT
788

GOE
08.03.01, 11.06.01

NOC
7343

O*NET-SOC
51-6041.00, 51-6042.00

glue, and nails and construct a pair of shoes from start to finish to the size and specifications of each customer.

During the industrial revolution, handmade shoes gradually were replaced by factory-made footwear. Machines could produce more shoes faster with fewer workers than was possible with traditional methods.

Around the middle of the 19th century, several changes took place in shoe manufacturing. In 1845, the rolling machine, an important labor-saving device for preparing leather, was invented. The following year, Elias Howe patented a sewing machine in the United States, which was adapted for use in stitching shoe uppers. In 1858, Lyman R. Blake patented a machine for sewing the parts of shoes together. In 1874, Charles Goodyear Jr. invented the welt stitcher, which made possible machine production of high-grade welt shoes.

With the application of power to these machines, shoemaking was revolutionized. Shoes now could be made very quickly and cheaply. Furthermore, manufacturers began to produce better-fitting, more comfortable shoes. Factories began to produce many kinds of footwear in large quantities, and it became much easier for ordinary people to own comfortable shoes of the proper size.

Today, shoes are available in countless styles and designs, and Americans are buying more shoes than ever—an average of four to five pairs every year. However, about 90 percent of these shoes are made overseas, in Taiwan, China, Korea, Brazil, and other countries where the cost of labor is less than in the United States. Since 1968, the number of Americans employed in the manufacture of footwear has declined steadily. Some companies, notably those that make specialty footwear, such as cowboy boots, work shoes, and quality athletic shoes, have factories in the United States.

THE JOB

Even with competition from imports, shoe factories in America still produce approximately 376 million pairs of shoes in thousands of styles every year. Most of this work is done on machines, although some work is performed by hand. A single pair of shoes may consist of as many as 280 different parts and require 150 different machine steps. Nearly all shoes are made in batches, not in individual pairs. These batches may consist of a dozen or more pairs of shoes, which are kept together through the entire manufacturing process to ensure that the shoes are consistent in color, texture, size, and pattern.

The leather on the top part of a pair of shoes starts out as tanned animal hides that the manufacturer purchases and keeps in storage.

Keeping track of these hides is the job of *upper-leather sorters,* who sort, grade, and issue the hides that will be cut into shoe uppers. The leather is spread out under a cutting machine, which stamps down and cuts the leather into the various sections used for the shoe. This machine, tended by *cut-out-and-marking-machine operators,* also marks patterns for stitching, beveling, and punching holes and eyelets. The workers take care to avoid the imperfections that are in each hide and to cut the leather against the grain to minimize stretching when the shoes are worn.

Next, the lining, tongue, toe, and other parts of the shoe are sewn together on machines operated by *standard machine stitchers.* Shoe parts may be attached by machine using glue, nails, staples, and other fasteners. Other workers taper leather edges, trim linings, flatten seams, and attach buckles or eyelets. The throat of the shoe is then laced together by *lacers.*

At this point the shoe upper is still mostly flat and is missing its insole (the inside sole, on which the foot rests), outsole (the outside sole), and heel. Before these are added, the shoe needs to be shaped and made into the proper shoe size. This is done using individually sized molds called lasts, which may be made of wood or plastic and are shaped like feet. The shoe upper and lining are steamed to soften the leather, and then they are secured to the lasts and stretched to conform to the last shape. *Lasters* perform this task, either by hand or with a lasting machine.

While this is being done, other workers prepare insoles, outsoles, and heels to be attached to the shoe uppers. They include *stock fitters,* who stamp rough forms for soles out of tanned hides, and *rounders,* who trim the rough soles to the proper size. Meanwhile, other workers may cut heel blanks out of wood, leather, or fiberboard, and glue strips of leather trim to the heels.

The insole is the first piece that is attached to the shoe upper. It will be sewn or glued on by thread lasters. Next, *bottom fillers* may insert foam filling between the insole and outsole to provide a cushion for the ball of the foot and an even surface for attaching the outsole. The outsole is then stitched to the shoe by the welt, or lip of leather, that runs along the outside of the shoe. Now the shoe can be removed from the last and made ready for finishing. Heels are nailed on by *heel-nailing-machine operators,* and any excess leather or glue is removed by *machine trimmers. Inkers* apply ink, stain, color, glaze, or wax to the shoe parts and along the seams to color and protect the shoe, after which *brushers* hold and turn the shoe against revolving brushes to clean and polish it. After a final inspection, the shoes are ready to pack and ship to stores. If shoes have come out of the manufacturing process damaged or unfit for sale, they are sent to *cobblers,* who may use hand tools and machines to fix defects.

For shoes made of rubber, plastic, fabric, or other material, the manufacturing process is approximately the same. However, the die that cuts out the basic shoe pieces usually is heated. Many layers of material can be cut at once because, unlike leather, the layers are uniform in color, texture, and thickness. Also, cementing and heating are used more often to join the pieces of nonleather shoes.

Custom shoemakers may assemble shoes by hand individually or they may modify manufactured shoes to meet the needs of individual customers.

Most shoe and leather repair work still is done by hand. However, the work of shoe repairers has been made easier by such technological innovations as power-operated equipment and the introduction of mass-produced replacement parts and decorative ornaments. The most frequently performed task of shoe repairers is replacing worn heels and soles. In small shops, a single worker may perform all the tasks necessary to repair an item, but in large shops, individual workers may be assigned specialized tasks. For example, sewing, trimming, buffing, and dyeing may be the duties of different workers called *pad hands.* However, most workers eventually move from one task to another to learn and master different skills.

When filling orders for customized products, workers first choose and check a piece of leather for texture, color, and strength. Then they place a pattern of the item being produced on the leather, trace the pattern onto the leather, cut the leather, and sew the pieces together.

Custom shoe workers also modify existing footwear for people with foot problems and special needs. They may prepare inserts, heel pads, and lifts based on plaster casts of customers' feet.

Shoe and leather workers use both hand tools and machines in their work. The most commonly used hand tools are knives, hammers, awls (used to punch holes in leather), and skivers (for splitting leather). Power-operated equipment includes sewing machines, heel nailing machines, hole punching machines, and sole stitchers.

Between 30 and 50 percent of shoe and leather repairers own their own shops. Shoe repairers who run their own establishments must be business-minded. In addition to actual repair work, they have managerial responsibility for estimating repair costs, preparing sales slips, keeping records, buying supplies, and receiving payments. They also may supervise their employees.

A few shoe repairers are employed in the shoe repair services of department stores, shoe stores, and cleaning plants. Other related types of workers include *leather stampers,* who imprint designs on

Workers manufacture athletic shoes on a production line. *(Corbis)*

leather goods, and custom leather products makers such as *harness makers, luggage makers,* and *saddle makers.*

REQUIREMENTS

High School
Although a high school diploma may not be required of applicants for jobs in this field, as more people apply for a shrinking number of positions, employers are increasingly likely to prefer those who have completed high school and have some experience in operating machines. High school courses in shop and sewing are desirable for people seeking work in this field. Other helpful courses include math, English, and art classes, where you may have the chance to work with leather to create your own projects.

Postsecondary Training
Shoe production workers usually are trained on the job. Beginners may go through in-house training programs operated by their employer, or they may start out in helper or apprenticeship positions and learn the skills they need as they assist experienced workers. The training period varies; for some kinds of tasks, training can last up to two years; other operations can be learned in much less time.

A few vocational schools offer courses in shoe and boot making. These courses, which last from six months to a year, can prepare workers to start out in positions with higher wages than those with no specialized training. Shoe and leather workers and repairers generally learn their craft on the job, either through in-house training programs or working as helpers to experienced craftspeople. Helpers generally begin by performing simple tasks and progress to more difficult projects such as cutting or sewing leather. Trainees generally become fully skilled in six months to two years, depending on their aptitude and dedication and the nature of the work.

Training programs for shoe repairers are offered under the provisions of the Manpower Development and Training Act. Many vocational and trade schools also provide courses in the area of shoe making and repair.

A limited number of schools offer vocational training in shoe repair and leather work. These programs may last from six months to one year and teach basic skills, including leather cutting, stitching, and dyeing. Students in these programs learn shoe construction, practice shoe repair, and study the fundamentals of running a small business. Graduates are encouraged to gain additional training by working with an experienced leather worker or repairer. National and regional associations also offer specialized training seminars and workshops in custom shoe making, shoe repair, and other leather work.

Other Requirements

Shoe repairers should have considerable manual dexterity, good hand-eye coordination, and general physical stamina. They also must have self-discipline in order to work with little supervision. Mechanical aptitude and manual dexterity are desirable for many jobs in the shoe industry. For workers who do custom work, artistic ability is important. Approximately half of the workers in the shoe industry belong to a union, such as the United Food and Commercial Workers International Union or UNITE HERE.

EXPLORING

Students may be able to find summer or part-time jobs in the shoe industry and thus gain valuable firsthand experience as maintenance workers or assistants to experienced shoe repairers or craftworkers. However, very few jobs are available for inexperienced people who want to work on a part-time or temporary basis. It may be possible to get an insider's view of this work by talking with someone employed in a production job in the shoe industry.

Shoe Trades Publications produces three magazines on the industry that may be helpful in learning about shoemaking: *Shoemaking Inter-*

national, Leather Manufacturer, and *Canadian Footwear Journal.* For more information, visit the website http://www.shoetrades.com.

EMPLOYERS

There are approximately 16,000 shoe and leather workers and repairers in the United States. Of that number, roughly 25 percent are self-employed. Self-employed workers own and operate small shoe repair shops or leather manufacturing companies.

Shoe industry workers are employed in a variety of settings across the country, from large factories owned by multinational corporations to small shops run as family businesses. Those who prefer to leave the production field may work in buying or selling shoes for a retail establishment.

STARTING OUT

Job seekers should apply directly to shoe factories that employ entry-level workers. The usual method of entering the shoe repair field is to be hired as a helper in a shoe repair shop that offers on-the-job training or some sort of apprenticeship program. Leads to specific jobs may be located through the local offices of the state employment service or newspaper classified ads. Graduates of vocational training programs often can get assistance in finding jobs through the career services office of the school they attended. State employment services also may list job openings.

ADVANCEMENT

In the shoe industry, advancement often involves learning new skills on more complex machines. It can take from six weeks to six months to become skilled at operating some processing machines. Skill in cutting shoe uppers may take up to two years to learn. Higher wages usually accompany a change to more complicated tasks.

Some people who begin as production workers move into positions as supervisors and managers in factories. Those with the right combination of skills may open their own shoe repair shops.

Shoe repair helpers begin doing such simple tasks as staining, brushing, and shining shoes. As they gain experience, they progress to more complex jobs. After approximately two years of apprenticeship, helpers who demonstrate ability and initiative can become qualified shoe repairers. Skilled craftsworkers employed in large shops may advance to become supervisors or managers. For those who open their own shops, hard work and friendly service usually translate into increased clientele and greater income.

EARNINGS

Limited information on earnings suggests that most new workers in the shoe industry start out at low wages, perhaps as low as the federal minimum wage level. According to the *Occupational Outlook Handbook,* shoe and leather workers and repairers earned a median hourly wage of $9.51 in 2004 (or $18,780 annually). The highest-paid shoe industry workers can earn $13.67 or more an hour (or $28,430 or more per year).

Often workers receive increases within a few months, after they have gained some experience and developed job skills. Many production workers with experience are paid piecework rates, meaning that their pay is related to how much work they produce. Their actual earnings vary greatly, depending on such factors as the company that employs them and the nature of the job they do.

Employees in large shops receive from one to four weeks' paid vacation and at least six paid holidays a year.

For many shoe industry workers who are union members, pay rates and benefits are set by agreements between the union and company management. Fringe benefits may include health and life insurance, employer contributions to pension plans, and paid vacation days.

WORK ENVIRONMENT

In many shoe factories, production workers generally work 35 hours a week or less. In companies that produce custom goods, the standard workweek is about 40 hours.

The work is not strenuous, but it can require stamina. Many workers are on their feet much of the time and many jobs involve repetitive tasks. Workers who are paid according to how much they produce have an incentive to work accurately and at a brisk pace.

Conditions in plants vary. Many factories have modern, air-conditioned, well-lighted work areas, but some older plants are not as comfortable. For the most part, hazards are few if safety precautions are followed. Because so much machinery is used, plants can be very noisy. Some workers are exposed to unpleasant odors from dyes, stains, and other chemicals.

Although some repair shops are crowded, noisy, poorly lit, and characterized by unpleasant odors, working conditions in large repair shops, shoe repair departments, and in more modern shoe service stores generally tend to be good. Most shoe repairers work eight hours a day for a five- or six-day week. Self-employed individuals work longer—often 10 hours a day.

OUTLOOK

The U.S. Department of Labor predicts that employment in the shoe manufacturing industry will decline through 2012. Foreign competition has resulted in many American shoe factories closing as the labor costs for the shoes they produced were too high compared to foreign manufacturers. In fact, the United States now exports raw materials for shoes to foreign countries where workers make shoes that are returned to be sold here. Ninety percent of shoes now are manufactured overseas.

Increased automation also is causing a decline in the number of workers needed in the shoe industry. Innovations in the shoe manufacturing process such as laser cutting of materials and computer aided design and manufacturing mean that far fewer workers are needed for many tasks, and few new jobs will open up in the future. Most job openings in this field will come about only as experienced workers retire, switch to other jobs, or otherwise leave.

Prospects are better for workers who make custom-built shoes or modify shoes for special needs. As the average age of Americans increases, more people will need special footwear, and the demand for molded and orthopedic shoes may increase.

FOR MORE INFORMATION

For statistical information on the footwear industry, contact
American Apparel and Footwear Association
1601 North Kent Street, Suite 1200
Arlington, VA 22209
Tel: 800-520-2262
http://www.apparelandfootwear.org

For information on the certification process, education courses, and general information on pedorthics, contact
Board for Certification in Pedorthics
2025 Woodlane Drive
St. Paul, MN 55125-2998
Tel: 888-530-2733
Email: info@cpeds.org
http://www.cpeds.org

Tailors and Dressmakers

QUICK FACTS

School Subjects
Art
Family and consumer science
Mathematics

Personal Skills
Artistic
Following instructions

Work Environment
Primarily indoors
Primarily one location

Minimum Education Level
High school diploma

Salary Range
$15,170 to $23,010 to
$36,780

Certification or Licensing
None available

Outlook
Decline

DOT
785

GOE
11.06.01

NOC
7342

O*NET-SOC
51-6052.00, 51-6052.01,
51-6052.02

OVERVIEW

Tailors and *dressmakers* cut, sew, mend, and alter clothing. Typically, tailors work only with menswear, such as suits, jackets, and coats, while dressmakers work with women's clothing, including dresses, blouses, suits, evening wear, wedding and bridesmaids' gowns, and sportswear. Tailors and dressmakers are employed in dressmaking and custom-tailor shops, department stores, and garment factories; others are self-employed. Tailors, dressmakers, and sewers hold about 53,000 jobs in the United States.

HISTORY

The practice of making and wearing clothing evolved from the need for warmth and protection from injury. For example, in prehistoric times, people wrapped themselves in the warm skins of animals they killed for food. Throughout history, men and women of all cultures and economic classes have made clothing.

Early clothing styles developed according to the climate of the geographical area: skirts and loose blouses of thin fabrics in warmer climates, pants and coats of heavier fabrics in cold climates. Religious customs and occupations also affected clothing styles. But as civilizations grew more and more advanced, clothing as necessity evolved into clothing as fashion.

The invention of the spinning wheel, in use in the 12th century, sped the process of making threads and yarns. With the invention of the two-bar loom, fabric making increased, styles became more detailed, and clothing became more widely available. Fabric production further increased with other inventions, such as the spinning jenny that could spin more than one thread at a time, power looms that ran on steam, and the cotton gin. The invention of the sewing machine tremendously sped the production of garments, although tailors and dressmakers were never completely replaced by machines.

During the industrial revolution, factories replaced craft shops. High-production apparel companies employed hundreds of workers. Employees worked 12- to 14-hour workdays for low hourly pay in crowded rooms with poor ventilation and lighting. The poor working conditions of these factories, known as sweatshops, led to the founding of the International Ladies Garment Workers Union in 1900 and the Amalgamated Clothing Workers of America in 1914; these unions protected workers' rights, ensured their safety, and led to greatly improved working conditions.

Today, the precise skills of tailors and dressmakers are still in demand at factories, stores, and small shops. The limited investment required to cut and sew garments, the wide availability of fabrics, and the demand for one-of-a-kind, tailor-made garments are factors that continue to provide opportunities for self-employed tailors and dressmakers.

THE JOB

Some tailors and dressmakers make garments from start to completion. In larger shops, however, each employee usually works on a specific task, such as measuring, patternmaking, cutting, fitting, or stitching. One worker, for example, may only sew in sleeves or pad lapels. Smaller shops may only measure and fit the garment, then send piecework to outside contractors. Some tailors and dressmakers specialize in one type of garment, such as suits or wedding gowns. Many also do alterations on factory-made clothing.

Tailors and dressmakers may run their own business, work in small shops, or work in the custom-tailoring section of large department stores. Some work out of their home. Retail clothing stores, specialty stores, bridal shops, and dry cleaners also employ tailors and dressmakers to do alterations.

Tailors and dressmakers first help customers choose the garment style and fabric, using their knowledge of the various types of fabrics. They take the customer's measurements, such as height, shoulder width, arm length, and waist, and they note any special figure

Tailors and dressmakers must have excellent dexterity and the ability to measure accurately. *(Corbis)*

problems. They may use ready-made paper patterns or make one of their own. The patterns are then placed on the fabric, and the fabric pieces are carefully cut. When the garment design is complex, or if there are special fitting problems, the tailor or dressmaker may cut the pattern from inexpensive muslin and fit it to the customer; any adjustments are then marked and transferred to the paper pattern before it is used to cut the actual garment fabric. The pieces are basted together first and then sewn by hand or machine. After one or two fittings, which confirm that the garment fits the customer properly, the tailor or dressmaker finishes the garment with hems, buttons, trim, and a final pressing.

Some tailors or dressmakers specialize in a certain aspect of the garment-making process. *Bushelers* work in factories to repair flaws and correct imperfect sewing in finished garments. *Shop tailors* have a detailed knowledge of special tailoring tasks. They use shears or a knife to trim and shape the edges of garments before sewing, attach shoulder pads, and sew linings in coats. *Skilled tailors* put fine stitching on lapels and pockets, make buttonholes, and sew on trim.

REQUIREMENTS

High School

While in high school, you should get as much experience as you can by taking any sewing, tailoring, and clothing classes offered by vocational or home economics departments. There are also a number of institutions that offer either on-site or home-study courses in sewing and dressmaking. Art classes in sketching and design are also helpful. Math classes, such as algebra and geometry, will help you hone your ability to work with numbers and to visualize shapes.

Postsecondary Training

Tailors and dressmakers must have at least a high school education, although employers prefer college graduates with advanced training in sewing, tailoring, draping, patternmaking, and design. A limited number of schools and colleges in the United States offer this type of training, including Philadelphia University, the Fashion Institute of Technology in New York City, and the Parsons School of Design, also in New York. Students who are interested in furthering their career, and perhaps expanding from tailoring into design, may want to consider studying in one of these specialized institutions. It is, however, entirely possible to enter this field without a college degree.

Other Requirements

Workers in this field must obviously have the ability to sew very well, both by hand and machine, follow directions, and measure accurately. In addition to these skills, tailors and dressmakers must have a good eye for color and style. They need to know how to communicate with and satisfy customers. Strong interpersonal skills will help tailors and dressmakers get and keep clients.

EXPLORING

Take sewing classes at school. Also, check with your local park district or fabric and craft stores—they often offer lessons year-round. Find summer or part-time employment at a local tailor shop. This will give you valuable work experience. Contact schools regarding their programs in fashion design. If their course descriptions sound interesting, take a class or two. You can also create and sew your own designs or offer your mending and alteration services to your family and friends. Finally, visit department stores, clothing specialty stores, and tailor's shops to observe workers involved in this field.

EMPLOYERS

Approximately 53,000 tailors, dressmakers, and sewers are employed in the United States. Those interested in high fashion should check out haute couture houses such as Chanel or Yves Saint Laurent. These industry giants deal with expensive fabrics and innovative designs. They also cater to a high level of clientele. Be prepared for stiff competition because such businesses will consider only the most experienced, highly skilled tailors and dressmakers.

Tailors and dressmakers employed at retail department stores make alterations on ready-to-wear clothing sold on the premises. They may perform a small task such as hemming pants or suit sleeves or a major project such as custom fitting a wedding dress.

In some cases, it is possible for tailors or dressmakers to start their own businesses by making clothes and taking orders from those who like their work. Capital needed to start such a venture is minimal, since the most important equipment, such as a sewing machine, iron and ironing board, scissors, and notions, are widely available and relatively inexpensive. Unless the tailor or dressmaker plans to operate a home-based business, however, he or she will need to rent shop space. Careful planning is needed to prepare for a self-owned tailoring or dressmaking business. Anyone running a business needs to learn bookkeeping, accounting, and how to keep and order supplies. A knowledge of marketing is important too, since the owner of a business must know how, when, and where to advertise in order to attract customers. Tailors or dressmakers planning to start their own business should check with their library or local government to learn what requirements, such as permits, apply. Finally, don't forget to consult established tailors and dressmakers to learn the tricks of the trade.

STARTING OUT

Custom-tailor shops or garment-manufacturing centers sometimes offer apprenticeships to students or recent graduates, which give them a start in the business. As a beginner you may also find work in related jobs, such as a sewer or alterer in a custom-tailoring or dressmaking shop, garment factory, dry-cleaning store, or department store. Apply directly to such companies and shops and monitor local newspaper ads for openings as well. Check with your high school's career center to see if it has any industry information or leads for part-time jobs. Trade schools and colleges that have programs in textiles or fashion often offer their students help with job placement.

ADVANCEMENT

Workers in this field usually start by performing simple tasks. As they gain more experience and their skills improve, they may be assigned to more difficult and complicated tasks. However, advancement in the industry is typically somewhat limited. In factories, a production worker might be promoted to the position of line supervisor. Tailors and dressmakers can move to a better shop that offers higher pay or open their own business.

Some workers may find that they have an eye for color and style and an aptitude for design. With further training at an appropriate college, these workers may find a successful career in fashion design and merchandising.

EARNINGS

Salaries for tailors and dressmakers vary widely, depending on experience, skill, and location. The median annual salary for tailors, dressmakers, and custom sewers reported by the U.S. Department of Labor in 2004 was $11.06, or $23,010 a year for full-time work. The lowest paid 10 percent earned less than $15,170 a year, while the highest paid 10 percent earned more than $36,780 annually.

Workers employed by large companies and retail stores receive benefits such as paid holidays and vacations, health insurance, and pension plans. They are often affiliated with the labor union UNITE HERE—which may offer additional benefits. Self-employed tailors and dressmakers and small-shop workers usually provide their own benefits.

WORK ENVIRONMENT

Tailors and dressmakers in large shops work 40 to 48 hours a week, sometimes including Saturdays. Union members usually work 35 to 40 hours a week. Those who run their own businesses often work longer hours. Spring and fall are usually the busiest times.

Since tailoring and dressmaking require a minimal investment, some tailors and dressmakers work out of their homes. Those who work in the larger apparel plants may find the conditions less pleasant. The noise of the machinery can be nerve-wracking, the dye from the fabric may be irritating to the eyes and the skin, and some factories are old and not well maintained.

Much of the work is done sitting down, in one location, and may include fine detail work that can be time consuming. The work may be tiring and tedious and occasionally can cause eyestrain. In some cases, tailors and dressmakers deal directly with customers, who may be either pleasant to interact with, or difficult and demanding.

This type of work, however, can be very satisfying to people who enjoy using their hands and skills to create something. It can be gratifying to complete a project properly, and many workers in this field take great pride in their workmanship.

OUTLOOK

According to the U.S. Department of Labor, employment prospects in this industry are expected to decline through 2012. Factors attributing to the decline include the low cost and ready availability of factory-made clothing and the invention of laborsaving machinery such as computerized sewing and cutting machines. In fact, automated machines are expected to replace many sewing jobs in the next decade. In addition, the apparel industry has declined domestically as many businesses choose to produce their items abroad, where labor is cheap and, many times, unregulated.

Tailors and dressmakers who do reliable and skillful work, however, particularly in the areas of mending and alterations, should be able to find employment. This industry is large, employing thousands of people. Many job openings will be created as current employees leave the workforce due to retirement or other reasons.

FOR MORE INFORMATION

For information on careers in the apparel-manufacturing industry, contact

American Apparel and Footwear Association
1601 North Kent Street, Suite 1200
Arlington, VA 22209
Tel: 800-520-2262
http://www.apparelandfootwear.org

This is a professional membership organization for custom tailors and designers.

Custom Tailors and Designers Association of America
19 Mantua Road

Mt. Royal, NJ 08061
Tel: 856-423-1621
http://www.ctda.com

For a listing of home-study institutions offering sewing and dress-making courses, contact
Distance Education and Training Council
1601 18th Street, NW
Washington, DC 20009
Tel: 202-234-5100
Email: Rob@detc.org
http://www.detc.org

For information packets on college classes in garment design and sewing, contact the following schools:
Fashion Institute of Design and Merchandising
919 South Grand Avenue
Los Angeles, CA 90015-1421
Tel: 800-624-1200
http://www.fidm.com

Fashion Institute of Technology
Seventh Avenue at 27th Street
New York, NY 10001-5992
Tel: 212-217-7999
Email: fitinfo@fitnyc.edu
http://www.fitnyc.edu

Parsons School of Design
66 Fifth Avenue
New York, NY 10011
Tel: 800-252-0852
http://www.parsons.edu

Philadelphia University
School House Lane and Henry Avenue
Philadelphia, PA 19144-5497
Tel: 215-951-2700
http://www.philau.edu

For career information, visit the following website:
Career Threads
http://careerthreads.com

Textile Workers

QUICK FACTS

School Subjects
Computer science
Technical/shop

Personal Skills
Following instructions
Mechanical/manipulative
Technical/scientific

Work Environment
Primarily indoors
Primarily one location

Minimum Education Level
Associate degree

Salary Range
$14,000 to $22,670 to
$45,000

Certification or Licensing
None available

Outlook
Decline

DOT
040

GOE
08.02.01, 08.03.02

NOC
2233, 9616

O*NET-SOC
51-6061.00, 51-6062.00,
51-6063.00, 51-6064.00

OVERVIEW

Textile workers prepare natural and synthetic fibers for spinning into yarn and manufacture yarn into textile products that are used in clothing, in household goods, and for many industrial purposes. Among the processes that these workers perform are cleaning, carding, combing, and spinning fibers; weaving, knitting, or bonding yarns and threads into textiles; and dyeing and finishing fabrics. Other textile workers may work in research, design, and development, creating new fibers and new ways to process them, or improving methods of converting fibers into textiles and textile products. Textile, apparel, and furnishings workers hold more than 1.1 million jobs in the United States.

HISTORY

Archaeological evidence suggests that people have been weaving natural fibers into cloth for at least 7,000 years. Basketweaving probably preceded and inspired the weaving of cloth. By about 5,000 years ago, cotton, silk, linen, and wool fabrics were being produced in several areas of the world. While ancient weavers used procedures and equipment that seem simple by today's standards, some of the cloth they made was of fine quality and striking beauty.

Over time, the production of textiles grew into a highly developed craft industry with various regional centers that were renowned for different kinds of textile products. Yet, until the 18th century, the making of fabrics was largely a cottage industry in which no more than a few people, often family groups, worked in small shops with their own equipment to make products by hand. With the industrial revolution and the invention of machines such as the cotton gin and the power loom, a wide variety of textiles could be produced in factories at low cost and in large quantities. Improvements have continued into the 20th century, so that today many processes in making textiles are highly automated.

Other changes have revolutionized the production of fabrics. The first attempts to make artificial fibers date to the 17th century, but it was not until the late 19th and early 20th centuries that a reasonably successful synthetic, a kind of rayon, was developed from the plant substance cellulose. Since then, hundreds of synthetic fibers have been developed from such sources as coal, wood, ammonia, and proteins. Other applications of science and technology to the textile industry have resulted in cloth that has a wide variety of attractive or useful qualities. Many fabrics that resist creases, repel stains, or are fireproof, mothproof, antiseptic, nonshrinking, glazed, softened, or stiff are the product of modern mechanical or chemical finishing.

Of the textiles produced in the United States today, only about half are used for wearing apparel. The rest are used in household products (towels, sheets, upholstery) and industrial products (conveyor belts, tire cords, parachutes).

THE JOB

Textile workers are employed in three major areas: research, design, and development; manufacturing and quality control; and customer service and sales.

Research, Design, Development, and Quality Control

Those involved in research and development study natural, manufactured, and synthetic fibers and textiles to determine their nature, origin, use, improvement, and processing methods. Natural fibers include wool, mohair, cashmere, camel's hair, alpaca, bristles, feathers, similar animal and fowl fibers, and plant fibers, such as cotton, linen, and jute. Manufactured fibers include nylon, polyester, olefin, and acrylic. *Research and development technicians,* sometimes called *assistant research scientists* or *assistant engineers,* study polymer science, fiber chemistry, yarn production, fabrication efficiency and flexibility, dyeing and finishing, development or modification of production machinery, and application of new technology to solve problems. Some research technicians develop new textiles to be used for a specific purpose, while others design new uses for existing textiles. *Product development technicians* work with research and development staff to develop prototypes of products. Technicians conduct performance tests on samples and combine them with use, wear, or product tests. These may include tests for tensile strength, abrasion resistance, washability, flammability, elasticity, and comfort using standard test methods and specialized testing equipment. Depending on test results, technicians may then modify the product.

Textile workers involved in quality control make sure that textile products meet or exceed standards and specifications, such as weight and count characteristics, colorfastness, and stability. These standards must be met in a safe, cost-effective, and efficient manner. *Quality control technicians, engineers,* and *managers* develop these standards and specifications and conduct tests to be sure that both purchased and produced items meet them. Quality control technicians also develop procedures for troubleshooting and problem solving in purchasing, product specification, or production. Quality control technicians need to understand the scientific principles behind textile products and must also know how to operate the manufacturing and testing equipment; at times, they must operate the machinery or perform the tests themselves. They may also teach new operators the procedures.

Manufacturing

Most textile workers in manufacturing operate or tend machines. In the most modern plants, the machines are often quite sophisticated and include computerized controls. Workers in textile manufacturing can be grouped in several categories. Some workers operate machines that clean and align fibers, draw and spin them into yarn, and knit, weave, or tuft the yarn into textile products. Other workers, usually employees of chemical companies, tend machines that produce synthetic fibers through chemical processes. Still other workers prepare machines before production runs. They set up the equipment, adjusting timing and control mechanisms, and they often maintain the machines as well. Another category of workers specializes in finishing textile products before they are sent out to consumers. The following paragraphs describe just a few of the many kinds of specialized workers in textile manufacturing occupations.

In the transformation of raw fiber into cloth, *staple cutters* may perform one of the first steps. They place opened bales of raw stock or cans of sliver (combed, untwisted strands of fiber) at the feed end of a cutting machine. They guide the raw stock or sliver onto a conveyor belt or feed rolls, which pull it against the cutting blades. They examine the cut fibers as they fall from the blades and measure them to make sure they are the required length.

Spinneret operators oversee machinery that makes manufactured fibers from such nonfibrous materials as metal or plastic. Chemical compounds are dissolved or melted in a liquid, which is then extruded, or forced, through holes in a metal plate, called a spinneret. The size and shape of the holes determine the shape and uses of the fiber. Workers adjust the flow of fiber base through the spinneret, repair breaks in the fiber, and make minor adjustments to the machinery.

Frame spinners, also called *spinning-frame tenders,* tend machines that draw out and twist the sliver into yarn. These workers patrol the spinning-machine area to ensure that the machines have a continuous supply of sliver or roving (a soft, slightly twisted strand of fiber made from sliver). They replace nearly empty packages of roving or sliver with full ones. If they detect a break in the yarn being spun, or in the roving or sliver being fed into the spinning frame, they stop the machine and repair the break. They are responsible for keeping a continuous length of material threaded through the spinning frame while the machine is operating.

Spinning supervisors supervise and coordinate the activities of the various spinning workers. From the production schedule, they determine the quantity and texture of yarn to be spun and the type of fiber to be used. Then they compute such factors as the proper spacing of rollers and the correct size of twist gears, using mathematical formulas and tables and their knowledge of spinning machine processes. As the spun yarn leaves the spinning frame, they examine it to detect variations from standards.

A textile production worker adjusts the tension on one of the rapier weaving machines. Once the fiber is spun into yarn or thread, it is ready for weaving, knitting, or tufting. Woven fabrics are made on looms that interlace the threads. Knit products, such as socks or women's hosiery, are produced by intermeshing loops of yarn. The tufting process, used in making carpets, involves pushing loops of yarn through a material backing.

Beam-warper tenders work at high-speed warpers, which are machines that automatically wind yarn onto beams, or cylinders, preparatory to dyeing or weaving. A creel, or rack of yarn spools, is positioned at the feed end of the machine. The workers examine the creel to make sure that the size, color, number, and arrangement of the yarn spools correspond to specifications. They thread the machine with the yarn from the spools, pulling the yarn through several sensing devices and fastening the yarn to the empty cylinder. After setting a counter to record the amount of yarn wound, they start the machine. If a strand of yarn breaks, the machine stops, and the tenders locate and tie the broken ends. When the specified amount of yarn has been wound, they stop the machine, cut the yarn strands, and tape the cut ends.

Weavers or *loom operators* operate a battery of automatic looms that weave yarn into cloth. They observe the cloth being woven carefully to detect any flaws, and they remove weaving defects by cutting out the filling (cross) threads in the area. If a loom stops, they locate the problem and either correct it or, in the case of mechanical breakdown, notify the appropriate repairer.

After the fabric is removed from the loom, it is ready for dyeing and finishing, which includes treating fabrics to make them fire-, shrink-, wrinkle-, or soil-resistant.

Dye-range operators control the feed end of a dye range, which is an arrangement of equipment that dyes and dries cloth. Operators position the cloth to be dyed and machine-sew its end to the end of the cloth already in the machine. They turn valves to admit dye from a mixing tank onto the dye pads, and they regulate the temperature of the dye and the air in the drying box. They start the machine, and when the process is complete, they record yardage dyed, lot numbers, and the machine running time. *Colorists, screen printing artists, screen makers,* and *screen printers* print designs on textiles.

Cloth testers perform tests on "gray goods"—raw, undyed, unfinished fabrics—and finished cloth samples. They may count the number of threads in a sample, test its tensile strength in a tearing machine, and crease it to determine its resilience. They may also test for such characteristics as abrasion resistance, fastness of dye, flame retardance, and absorbency, depending on the type of cloth.

Customer Service and Sales
Workers in customer service and sales act as liaisons between manufacturers and the buyers of their textiles and clothing. They make sure the textiles meet specifications and are delivered in the most timely, cost-effective way. *Customer sales and service technicians* have an intimate knowledge of production and quality control, as well as good communication skills. They have to understand customer needs and convey them to research and development or production personnel. They may be required to travel.

REQUIREMENTS

High School
Students who are interested in careers in research and development/ quality control should get a strong background in mathematics by taking at least two years of math classes, including algebra and geometry. Take computer courses that will allow you to become familiar with this tool. Science classes that involve laboratory work, such as physics, chemistry, and biology, will give you an educational edge as well as allow you to experience working in a lab environment. Also,

take mechanical drafting and design courses. These courses will give you the opportunity to work with blueprints and learn the basics of design. Finally, don't skimp on English classes. Four years of English courses will give you a solid background in researching and writing, two skills you will need throughout your career.

If you are interested in working in textile manufacturing, take courses in physics, chemistry, mathematics, and English. Computer skills are necessary, since many machines are now operated by computer technology.

A good liberal arts education in high school will prepare you for a career in customer service and sales in the textile industry. Take English, speech, psychology, business, and marketing classes. Computer science will also be useful since computers are an integral tool for customer service and sales workers in any industry.

Postsecondary Training

In past years, textile workers typically prepared for this career by receiving on-the-job training. Although this may still happen occasionally, most companies today want to hire graduates of a two-year college or technical school with a degree in a textile-related field. Some companies even require a four-year degree. Several schools, especially in the Southeast, have four-year degree programs in textile technology, textile engineering, textile management/production/service, textile design, textile chemistry, fiber/textiles/weaving. A bachelor of science degree in physical sciences, chemistry, or science technologies can also provide the appropriate skills and knowledge for those seeking careers in research and development/quality control. Major centers for textile education include North Carolina State University in Raleigh; the Center for Applied Textile Technology in Belmont, Georgia; the Institute of Technology in Atlanta, Georgia; Clemson University in South Carolina; and Philadelphia College of Textiles and Science. Students who are interested in working in customer services or sales might consider pursuing associate or bachelor's degrees in textile marketing, business, or a related field.

Other Requirements

In addition to educational requirements, certain personal qualifications are needed to be successful, including the ability to work with others and to accept supervision, to work independently and accept responsibility for your work, and to work accurately and carefully. Requirements vary by job specialty. For example, machine operators need physical stamina, manual dexterity, and a mechanical aptitude to do their job. Those in research and development/quality control need strong communication skills to be able to communicate with workers and customers from different cultures and educational backgrounds. They also need strong analytical skills, an attentiveness to detail, and strong organizational skills.

EXPLORING

Ask your guidance counselor to contact the National Council of Textile Organizations for descriptive materials and audiovisual presentations on the textile industry. Also, you or your guidance counselor should try contacting individual companies for informative brochures about their employment opportunities. Ask your counselor to help arrange a visit to a producing textile or clothing factory where you can observe the machinery and work. You may also be able to speak to some of the workers there and gain insight about the work. Consider joining a science club that offers the opportunity to work on projects involving laboratory work and experimentation. One of the best ways for you to explore the field is to get a summer job with a textile or apparel company. Although your work may not involve activities closely related to the actual production operations, you will still benefit from working in this environment and may also make contacts in the field. Ask the people you work with about their jobs, their educational backgrounds, what they see for the future in this field, and any other questions you may have.

EMPLOYERS

The Southeast, principally North Carolina, South Carolina, and Georgia, has more than 60 percent of the textile jobs. The remaining jobs in the United States are found almost exclusively in the South, the Northeast, and California. Workers can find employment in research institutions, textile manufacturing plants, product design and development companies, raw materials manufacturers, testing facilities, apparel companies, and manufacturers of home furnishings. Companies need not necessarily be textile based, however, to have opportunities for textile workers. There are also many jobs in industrial settings, such as the automotive industry, chemical companies that make binders for textiles, and biomedical companies that make textiles for a variety of uses in the health care field.

After accumulating a great deal of experience and knowledge in textiles, those involved in research, development of new products, or design of textiles and products can become independent consultants. They basically work for themselves and provide services to small- and medium-sized firms.

STARTING OUT

Graduate textile workers are often hired by recruiters from the major employers in the field. Recruiters regularly visit schools with textile programs and arrange interviews with graduating students through the school's career services center.

Some students, however, attend school under the sponsorship of a textile or clothing company and usually go to work for their sponsor after graduation. Some are cooperative students who attend school with the understanding that they will return to their sponsor plant. Some sponsoring companies, however, do not place any restriction on their co-op students and allow them to find the best job they can with any company. Students may also write to or visit potential employers that are of special interest.

Some textile workers obtain jobs by answering newspaper advertisements or by applying directly to the personnel office of a textile plant. A new worker usually receives between a week and several months of on-the-job training, depending on the complexity of the job.

ADVANCEMENT

Advancement opportunities for textile workers vary by specialty. Laboratory workers may advance to supervisory positions in the lab. If their educational background includes such courses as industrial engineering and quality control, they may move up to management jobs where they plan and control production. Production workers in textile manufacturing who become skilled machine operators may be promoted to positions in which they train new employees. Other workers can qualify for better jobs by learning additional machine-operating skills. Usually the workers with the best knowledge of machine operations are those who set up and prepare machines before production runs. Skilled workers who show that they have good judgment and leadership abilities may be promoted to supervisory positions, in charge of a bank of machines or a stage in the production process. Workers in sales and customer service may advance by taking on more responsibilities or by being asked to manage coworkers or other departments.

EARNINGS

Earnings of textile workers vary depending on the type of plant where they are employed and the workers' job responsibilities, the shift they work, and seniority. Workers at plants located in the North tend to be paid more than those in the South.

According to the U.S. Department of Labor, median salaries for full-time textile workers ranged from $14,000 to $33,000 annually in 2004. Median hourly wages of textile cutting machine setters, operators, and tenders were $10.22 (or $21,260 annually) in 2004. Textile knitting and weaving machine setters, operators, and tenders earned $11.46 an hour (or $23,840 annually). Textile winding, twisting, and drawing out machine setters, operators, and tenders earned $10.90 an hour (or $22,670 annually). Textile bleaching and dyeing machine operators and tenders earned $10.76 an hour (or $22,390 annually). Textile employees with supervisory responsibilities can make more than $45,000 a year.

Most workers with a year or more of service receive paid vacations and insurance benefits. Many are able to participate in pension plans, profit sharing, or year-end bonuses. Some companies offer their employees discounts on the textiles or textile products they sell.

WORK ENVIRONMENT

The textile industry of today is comparatively safe and grows more comfortable every year. Modern textile plants have temperature and humidity controls that outdo those in most homes and apartments. Machines now handle most of the heavy lifting. Workers often are required to wear protective face masks, earplugs, and protective clothing. The new plant is typically a one-story building, clean, well-lighted, smaller than its counterpart of a few years ago, and much more efficient. The industry places great emphasis on safety, cleanliness, and orderliness.

Workweeks in this industry average 40 hours in length. Depending on business conditions, some plants may operate 24 hours a day, with three shifts a day. Production employees may work rotating shifts, so that they share night and weekend hours. Some companies have a four-shift continuous operating schedule, consisting of a 168-hour workweek made of up of four daily shifts totaling 42 hours a week. This system offers a rotating arrangement of days off. During production cutbacks, companies may go to a three- or four-day workweek, but they generally try to avoid layoffs during slow seasons.

OUTLOOK

The U.S. Department of Labor predicts a decline in employment for this field through 2012, even as the demand for textile products increases. Changes in the textile industry will account for much of this decline. Factories are reorganizing production operations for greater efficiency and installing equipment that relies on more highly automated and computerized machines and processes. Such technology as shuttleless and air-jet looms and computer-controlled machinery allows several machines to be operated by one operator while still increasing speed and productivity.

Another factor that will probably contribute to a reduced demand for U.S. textile workers is an increase in imports of textiles from other countries. There is a continuing trend toward freer world markets and looser trade restrictions.

While fewer workers will be needed, there will continue to be many job openings each year as experienced people transfer to other jobs or leave the workforce. Education is increasingly important to employers trying to fill the small number of positions. High school graduates will likely be passed over in favor of applicants with at least two years, and preferably four years, of training.

FOR MORE INFORMATION

This national trade association for the U.S. textile industry has member companies in more than 30 states that process about 80 percent of all textile fibers consumed by plants in the United States. It works to encourage global competitiveness and increase foreign market access.

National Council of Textile Organizations
910 17th Street, NW, Suite 1020
Tel: 202-822-8028
Washington, DC 20006
http://www.ncto.org

The following research and graduate education organization offers a master's degree in textile technology and provides fee-based library and information services:

Institute of Textile Technology
North Carolina State University
College of Textiles
2401 Research Drive, Box 8301
Raleigh, NC 27695
http://www.itt.edu

For information on degree and continuing education programs in textile technology, contact

North Carolina Center for Applied Textile Technology
7220 Wilkinson Boulevard
Belmont, NC 28012

Tel: 704-825-3737
Email: info@nccatt.org

This union fights for workers' rights and represents workers in various industries, including basic apparel and textiles.
UNITE HERE
275 Seventh Avenue
New York, NY 10001-6708
Tel: 212-265-7000
http://www.unitehere.org

For career information, visit the following website
Career Threads
http://careerthreads.com

Index

Entries and page numbers in **bold** indicate major treatment of a topic.

A

AACS (American Association of Cosmetology Schools) 35
AICI (Association of Image Consultants International) 21, 24, 26–27
Amalgamated Clothing Workers of America 7, 177
American Federation of Television and Radio Artists (AFTRA) 152
American Jewelry Design Council 118
American Purchasing Society 52
apparel industry 1–3
 See also apparel industry workers
apparel industry workers 6–17
 advancement 13–14
 earnings 14
 employers 12
 exploring 12
 high school requirements 11
 history 6–8
 information on 17
 job, described 8–11
 outlook 15–16
 postsecondary training 11
 requirements 11–12
 starting out 12–13
 work environment 15
apparel inspectors 10
Aria 86
Armani, Georgio 68
artists' models 144
 See also models
ASC (Association of Stylists and Coordinators) 104, 106, 107
assemblers 8
assistant designers 69
 See also fashion designers
ATC (Agreement on Textiles and Clothing) 16

B

Bakst 41
barbers 28–29

Barkan, Helen 165–166
Barran, John 7
Bartolome, Emily 86, 87, 88, 90
beam-warper tenders 187
Beard, Thomas 167
beauticians. *See* cosmetologists
Berain, Jean 40
Bertin, Rose 64
Blake, Lyman R. 168
Boquet, Louis-Rene 40
bottom fillers 169
brushers 169
Burnacini 40
bushelers 178
buyers 65

C

Canadian Footwear Journal 173
casting stylists 102
CBI (Caribbean Basin Initiative) 16
Chesterfield, Earl of 157
cloth testers 188
cobblers 170
color analysts 18–24
 advancement 22
 earnings 22–23
 employers 22
 exploring 21
 high school requirements 20
 information on 24
 job, described 19–20
 outlook 23–24
 postsecondary training 20–21
 requirements 20–21
 starting out 22
 work environment 23
Color Designers International 27
colorists 188
Color Me Beautiful 19, 20, 21, 22
Color Me Beautiful (Jackson) 19, 21
Color Me Beautiful's Looking Your Best (Spillane and Sherlock) 18, 21
cosmetologists 2, 28–39
 advancement 36
 earnings 36–37
 employers 35

exploring 34–35
high school requirements 32
history 28–29
information on 38–39
job, described 29–32
outlook 38
overview 28
postsecondary training 32–34
requirements 32–34
starting out 35
work environment 37–38
costume designers 40–48
　advancement 44
　earnings 45–46
　employers 44
　exploring 43
　high school requirements 42–43
　history 40–41
　information on 47
　job, described 41
　outlook 46–47
　overview 40
　postsecondary training 43
　requirements 42–43
　starting out 44
　work environment 46
The Costume Designer's Handbook
　(Ingham and Covey) 43
Covey, Liz 43
customer sales and service technicians
　188
custom shoemakers 170
　See also shoe industry workers
cut-out-and-marking-machine opera-
　tors 169
cutters 8, 13–14

D
Daguerre, Louis 93
Dagyr, John Adam 167
DeBré, Greg 99–100
designers 3
design industry 2
diamond merchants 124
diamond workers 119
Direct Selling Women's Alliance 24
dressers 58
dressmakers 3, 176–183
　advancement 181
　earnings 181

employers 180
exploring 179–180
high school requirements 179
history 176–177
information on 182–183
job, defined 177–179
outlook 182
overview 176
postsecondary training 179
requirements 179
starting out 180–181
work environment 181–182
drying-machine operators 129
dye-range operators 188
dye-tub operators 129

E
Eastman, George 93, 143
editorial assistants 113
editor-in-chief 114
Elite Modeling Agency 89
estheticians. *See* cosmetologists

F
fact checkers 111
fashion authors 110–111
　See also fashion writers
fashion buyers 49–55
　advancement 53
　earnings 53–54
　employers 52
　exploring 52
　high school requirements 51
　history 49
　information on 54–55
　job, described 49–51
　outlook 54
　overview 49
　postsecondary training 51
　requirements 51–52
　starting out 52–53
　work environment 54
fashion coordinators 2, 56–63
　advancement 61
　earnings 61
　employers 60
　exploring 60
　high school requirements 58–59
　history 56–57
　information on 62–63

job, described 57–58
outlook 62
overview 56
postsecondary training 59
requirements 58–59
starting out 60–61
work environment 61–62
fashion correspondents 110–111
    See also fashion writers
fashion designers 2, **64–78**
advancement 69–70
earnings 70
employers 68–69
exploring 68
high school requirements 67
history 64–65
information on 71–72
job, described 65–66
outlook 71
overview 64
postsecondary training 67–68
requirements 67–68
starting out 69
work environment 70
fashion editors **110–116**
advancement 113–114
earnings 114
employers 112
exploring 112
high school requirements 111–112
history 110
information on 115–116
job, described 110–111
outlook 115
postsecondary training 112
requirements 111–112
starting out 113
work environment 114–115
fashion forecasters 61
Fashion Group International 27
fashion illustrators 2, **79–84**
advancement 82
books on 81
earnings 82–83
employers 82
exploring 81–82
high school requirements 80
history 79
information on 83–84
job, described 79–80

outlook 83
overview 79
postsecondary training 80–81
requirements 80–81
starting out 82
work environment 83
Fashion Institute of Technology 51,
    60, 104, 179
fashion merchandisers **49–55**
advancement 53
earnings 53–54
employers 52
exploring 52
high school requirements 51
history 49
information on 54–55
job, described 49–51
outlook 54
overview 49
postsecondary training 51
requirements 51–52
starting out 52–53
work environment 54
fashion model agents 2, **85–92**
advancement 90
earnings 91
employers 89–90
exploring 89
high school requirements 88
history 85–86
information on 92
job, described 86–88
outlook 92
overview 85
postsecondary training 88
requirements 88–89
starting out 90
work environment 91
fashion models 65, 143, 144, 145–
146
    See also models
fashion photographers **93–100**
advancement 97
books on 96
earnings 97–98
employers 96
exploring 95–96
high school requirements 94–95
history 93–94
information on 98–99

job, described 94
  outlook 98
  overview 93
  postsecondary training 95
  requirements 94–95
  starting out 96–97
  work environment 98
fashion publications 113
  See also specific publications
fashion reporters 110–111
  See also fashion writers
fashion stylists 101–109
  advancement 106–107
  earnings 107
  employers 105
  exploring 105
  high school requirements 103–104
  history 101–102
  information on 109
  job, described 102–103
  outlook 108–109
  overview 101
  postsecondary training 104
  requirements 103–105
  starting out 105–106
  work environment 107–108
fashion writers 110–116
  advancement 113–114
  earnings 114
  employers 112
  exploring 112
  high school requirements 111–112
  history 110
  information on 115–116
  job, described 110–111
  outlook 115
  postsecondary training 112
  requirements 111–112
  starting out 113
  work environment 114–115
Felix & Agatha 73
Fignar, Susan 19–20, 21, 22–24, 23
floor models 152
Ford, Eileen 86
Ford, Jerry 86
Ford Models Inc. 86, 89
frame spinners 187
full-fashioned garment knitters 130

G
garment steamer 129
Gellatly, Marion 24–27
gem cutters 117, 119
gemologists 117
Giovagnoli, Melissa 21
Glamour 80, 94
Goodyear, Charles Jr. 168

H
hairdressers 58
  See also cosmetologists; hair stylists
hair stylists 102
  See also cosmetologists
hand sewers 10, 15, 16
harness makers 171
Harper's Bazaar 157
head of stock 52
heel-nailing-machine operators 169
High School of Fashion Industries 58–59
Howe, Elias 6, 64, 168
Hutton, Lauren 86

I
IATSE (International Alliance of Theatrical Stage Employees) 139
illustrators 79
image consultants 18–27
  advancement 22
  earnings 22–23
  employers 22
  exploring 21
  high school requirements 20
  information on 24
  job, described 19–20
  outlook 23–24
  postsecondary training 20–21
  requirements 20–21
  starting out 22
  work environment 23
Image Consulting: The New Career (Timberlake) 21
IMG 89
industrial models 143
Ingham, Rosemary 43
inkers 169
International Ladies' Garment Workers' Union 7, 177

J

Jackson, Carole 19, 21
Jacquard-plate makers 128
jeweler managers 124
jewelers 117–126
  advancement 123–124
  earnings 124
  employers 122
  exploring 122
  high school requirements 120–121
  history 117–118
  information on 125–126
  job, described 118–120
  outlook 125
  overview 117
  postsecondary training 120–121
  requirements 120–121
  starting out 123
  work environment 124–125
Jewelers of America 121
jewelry appraisers 120
jewelry artists 118
jewelry buyers 120
jewelry engravers 119
jewelry repairers 117–126
  advancement 123–124
  earnings 124
  employers 122
  exploring 122
  high school requirements 120–121
  history 117–118
  information on 125–126
  job, described 118–120
  outlook 125
  overview 117
  postsecondary training 120–121
  requirements 120–121
  starting out 123
  work environment 124–125
jewelry sales staff 120

K

Karan, Donna 68
knit goods industry workers 127–135
  advancement 132–133
  earnings 133
  employers 132
  exploring 132
  high school requirements 130–131

history 127
  information on 134–135
  job, described 128–130
  outlook 134
  overview 127
  postsecondary training 131
  requirements 130–132
  starting out 132
  work environment 133–134
knit-goods washer 129
knit-machine cutters 129
knit-pattern assemblers 128
knit-pattern markers 129
knit-pattern wheel makers 128
knitter mechanics 128
knitting-machine fixers 129

L

lacers 169
lasters 169
layout workers 14
Leather Manufacturer 173
leather repairers. *See* shoe industry
  workers
leather stampers 170–171
leather workers 170–171
  See also shoe industry workers
loom operators 187–188
loopers 130
luggage makers 171

M

machine trimmers 169
makeup artists 2, 58, 136–142
  advancement 140
  earnings 140–141
  employers 139
  exploring 139
  high school requirements 137–138
  history 136–137
  information on 142
  job, described 137
  outlook 141–142
  overview 136
  postsecondary training 138
  requirements 137–139
  starting out 140
  work environment 141
makeup stylists 102

managing editors 114
manicurists. *See* nail technicians
markers 8
Mathis, Darlene 21
Mehrabian, Albert 18
merchandise managers 53
modeling agents 58
models 2, **143–155**
  advancement 151
  books on 148
  earnings 151–153
  employers 149
  exploring 149
  high school requirements 146
  history 143–144
  information on 154–155
  job, described 144–146
  outlook 154
  overview 143
  postsecondary training 146
  requirements 146–149
  starting out 150
  work environment 153–154
Montague, Lady Mary Worley 156–157

N
NAFTA (North American Free Trade
  Agreement) 2, 16
nail artists. *See* nail technicians
nail sculpturists. *See* nail technicians
nail technicians 2, **156–166**
  advancement 163–164
  earnings 164
  employers 162–163
  by ethnicity 163
  exploring 162
  high school requirements 159–160
  history 156–158
  industry statistics on 158
  information on 166
  job, described 158–159
  outlook 165–166
  overview 156
  postsecondary training 160–161
  requirements 159–162
  starting out 163
  work environment 164–165
  See also cosmetologists
National Association of Purchasing
  Management 51, 52

National Council of Textile Organizations 190
*Networlding: Building Relation-
  ships and Opportunities for Success*
  (Giovagnoli) 21

O
off-figure stylists 102
on-figure stylists 102
orthopedic shoe designers. *See* shoe
  industry workers
orthopedic shoe makers. *See* shoe
  industry workers
overedge sewers 130

P
pad hands 170
Parsons School of Design 179
patternmakers 13, 14
pedicurists. *See* nail technicians
Philadelphia University 179
photographers 2, 3
photographic models. *See* models
photo stylists. *See* fashion stylists
Pivot Point International 161
planners 58
plant managers 14
plant safety experts 14
plant training specialists 14
Powerful Presence 24
pressers 10, 14
press representatives 65
product demonstrators 143
product developers 58, 61
product development technicians
  185
production control technicians 10
production superintendents 14
production workers 58
product promoters 143, 145
Professional Photographers of America 95
publications, fashion 113
  See also specific publications
Publishers Weekly 113

R
Redbook 80, 94
Reece Machinery Company 7
researchers 111

Revlon 86, 157, 158
rounders 169

S

saddle makers 171
sampling demonstration models 145
Schultze, Johann H. 93
Screen Actors Guild (SAG) 150, 152
screen makers 188
screen printers 188
screen printing artists 188
section supervisors 14
Seventeen 89, 94
sewers 9, 14
sewing machine operators 9–10, 130
S. Fignar & Associates Inc. 19
Sherlock, Christine 18, 19, 20, 21, 22, 23
shoe industry workers 167–175
    advancement 173–174
    earnings 174
    employers 173
    exploring 172–173
    high school requirements 171
    history 167–168
    information on 175
    job, described 168–171
    outlook 175
    overview 167
    postsecondary training 171–172
    requirements 171–172
    starting out 173
    work environment 174–175
Shoemaking International 172–173
shoe repairers 170, 172, 173
    See also shoe industry workers
shoppers 44
shop tailors 178–179
Shrimpton, Jean 85
silversmiths 119
Singer, Isaac 7
skilled tailors 179
soft-goods stylists 102
specialty models 145
Spillane, Mary 18, 21
spinneret operators 186–187
spinning-frame tenders 187
spinning supervisors 187
spreaders 8
standard machine stitchers 169

staple cutters 186
stock fitters 169
stylists 2, 3, 58, 61
Swan, Kathryn 73–74

T

tailors 3, 10, 13, 14, 16, **176–183**
    advancement 181
    earnings 181
    employers 180
    exploring 179–180
    high school requirements 179
    history 176–177
    information on 182–183
    job, defined 177–179
    outlook 182
    overview 176
    postsecondary training 179
    requirements 179
    starting out 180–181
    work environment 181–182
Taylor, Elizabeth 157
textile assistant engineers 185
textile assistant research scientists 185
textile engineers 186
textile industry 1
    See also textile workers
textile managers 186
textile quality control technicians 186
textile research and development technicians 185
textile workers 184–194
    advancement 191
    earnings 191–192
    employers 190
    exploring 190
    high school requirements 188–189
    history 184–185
    information on 193–194
    job, described 185–188
    outlook 192–193
    overview 184
    postsecondary training 189
    requirements 188–190
    starting out 191
    work environment 192
Thimonnier, Barthelemy 6
Thousand, Karol 31–32, 33
Timberlake, Joan 21
toppers 130

Torelli 40
trend forecasters 58
Triangle Shirtwaist Factory 7
tubular-splitting-machine tender 129
Twiggy 85

U
UNITE HERE 132
UNITE (Union of Needle Trades
  Industrial and Textile Employees) 7
University of Cincinnati 75–77, 78
upper-leather sorters 169
USA (United Scenic Artists) 43, 45, 48

V
Varushka 85
Victoria's Secret 62

Voelker-Ferrier, Margaret 75–78
Vogue 80, 89, 157

W
watchmakers 119
weavers, weaving 127, 187–188
  See also textile workers
websites, useful 45
Wilhelmina 89
Women of Color (Mathis) 21
Women's Wear Daily 68, 80, 89, 94
Woodyard, Sean 30–31, 32, 38
Worth, Charles Frederick 64–65, 143

Z
Zuckerman, Pam 60–61